How to Use an Interactive Whiteboard Really Effectively in Your Secondary Classroom

Also available:

How to Use an Interactive Whiteboard Really Effectively in Your Primary Classroom,
Jenny Gage (ISBN 1-84312-235-9)

Teaching the National ICT Strategy at Key Stage 3: A Practical Guide,
Clare Furlonger and Susan Haywood (ISBN 1-84312-029-1)

ICT for Teaching Assistants,
John Galloway (ISBN 1-84312-203-0)

How to Use an Interactive Whiteboard Really Effectively in Your Secondary Classroom

Jenny Gage

David Fulton Publishers

David Fulton Publishers Ltd
The Chiswick Centre, 414 Chiswick High Road, London W4 5TF

www.fultonpublishers.co.uk

First published in Great Britain in 2006 by David Fulton Publishers
David Fulton Publishers is a division of Granada Learning Ltd, part of ITV plc.

10 9 8 7 6 5 4 3 2 1

Note: The right of Jenny Gage to be identified as the author of this work has been asserted
by her in accordance with the Copyright, Designs and Patents Act 1988.

Copyright © Jenny Gage 2006

British Library Cataloguing in Publication Data
A catalogue record for this book is available from the British Library.

ISBN 1 84312 262 6

Typeset by Servis Filmsetting Ltd, Manchester
Printed and bound in Great Britain

Contents

To Eileen Furby

a fantastic head of department, who first gave me the opportunity and encouragement to explore using ICT in my teaching

Acknowledgements

I am very grateful to the head teacher and staff of Parkside Community College, Cambridge, where I was able to observe many excellent lessons involving an interactive whiteboard. I would particularly like to thank Fran Wilson whose help in setting up and organising my visit was invaluable. I would also like to thank the following teachers from Cambridge, Edinburgh, Jersey, Northampton and Norwich for their help: Francis Chalmers, Steve Cox, Mike Cripps, Joe Dhesi, James Durran, Francis Farrell, Jenny Griffiths, Tim Holden, Andrina Inglis, Hanan McKeand, Rory Steel and Hilary Tunnicliffe.

Michele Conway of Cambridge-Hitachi, and Hayato Fujigaki and Peter Kerrison of Hitachi Software Engineering (UK) Ltd showed me what the StarBoard can do, and patiently answered all my questions about it. Any mistakes in any of the instructions, both for the StarBoard and for all other software described, are mine.

Thanks also go to John Galloway and Chris Drage for their contributions to this book.

Helen and Robert, my niece and nephew, told me of their experiences at school with the interactive whiteboard and provided me with raw material for some of the resources. Susannah Crockford gave me suggestions for annotating English texts.

Finally, I want to thank my husband Andrew, whose suggestions and proofreading were, as always, a great help, and whose cooking and shopping helped me to complete this book more or less on time.

Foreword

In 2003, when the mere mention of an interactive whiteboard (IWB) brought a flutter to the heart of every ever-hopeful, hard-pressed ICT co-ordinator, Stephen Twigg, the then Minister for Schools, announced the provision of £25 million for the purchase of IWBs for schools. The following January, the then Secretary of State for Education, Charles Clarke, announced a further £25 million to be made available. The total £50 million was split between primary and secondary sectors, and secondaries were equipped with a department's worth of 'free' IWBs, projectors and speakers. Enterprising schools, such as the technology college in which I work, didn't miss the opportunity. My college chose a department with the most number of rooms, thus gaining the maximum number of 'freebies' allowed!

All this investment was due – it was explained by the Secretary of State at BETT 2004 – to studies undertaken at several universities up and down the country, each of which concluded that teaching with IWBs resulted in more focused learning and more students on-task than is usually the case otherwise. As if to underline the importance of the initiative and to provide an added incentive, the DfES has introduced new flexibilities on the use of Devolved Formula Capital Funding, from which schools are able, should they deem it a priority, to purchase ICT infrastructure and equipment, including interactive whiteboards, the rationale being that schools are best placed to decide where the money is spent and allow local solutions to be matched to local needs and priorities. Hands up how many of you are working in schools where, during a heavy shower, the water runs down your lovely new IWB because money was diverted away from the proposed new roof job! All this government spending and recent focus on interactive technologies must surely have some substance. There must be something in it.

In February 2005, the DfES published the 14–19 Education and Skills White Paper in which it sets out the importance of the use of interactive whiteboards in improving teaching and learning opportunities across the whole curriculum. It points out that the integration of the IWB encourages teachers to manipulate the technology in order to encourage and develop active learning and extend the range of teaching styles. It also emphasises the importance of whole-class teaching strategies including teacher modelling and demonstration, prompting, probing, promoting questioning, managed whole-class discussion, reviewing of work in progress to reinforce key points emerging from individual and group work, and whole-class evaluation in plenary sessions.

The White Paper concludes that interactive whiteboards are powerful teaching tools that have the potential to:

⊙ enhance demonstration and modelling;

⊙ improve the quality of interactions and teacher assessment through the promotion of effective questioning;

⊙ redress the balance of making resources and planning for teaching; and

⊙ increase the pace and depth of learning.

One point deserves to be stressed from the outset: an IWB in the hands of a mediocre teacher is only going to offer mediocre learning experiences. In the hands of a skilled, imaginative and dedicated teacher learning and engagement are limitless. Technology, no matter how advanced, is never going to replace a good teacher; it can only enhance and extend teachers' skills and abilities. If you have any doubts about why you should be involved, just consider that children today live in a fast-moving, multimedia world where change is the norm. As teachers, we have to compete for their attention and their engagement; we have to embrace and use every opportunity to get and hold that attention. As teachers already using interactive technologies successfully in their classrooms have found, learning can acquire a new rigour and pace, with students actually competing to get to the front of the classroom in order that they get to interact first!

There is now an extensive range of commercial and non-commercial digital resources that teachers can use to enhance teaching and learning. E-learning credits (eLCs) are available to help schools purchase high-quality, curriculum-specific resources, and the pedagogical quality of the packages available continues to improve. Teachers do not need to spend as much time creating their own resources but they do need to know where to find them, how to adapt them for their own lessons and how to develop their teaching strategies to exploit them.

This book sets out to provide you, the teacher, with practical help and assistance in understanding the IWB and explains how it can do for you what it seems to be doing for your colleague along the corridor. It offers practical, hands-on tutorials and advice on the best use of IWB software tools. It also provides advice on choosing, purchasing and installing an IWB, not because it assumes that you, personally, might have to make important resourcing decisions for your department/school, but that you are informed enough to be able to influence the decisions made by others through understanding what you need in terms of hardware/software provision in order to do the job effectively. Most importantly, it looks at what you need to consider when integrating the new technology into classroom practice, including an outline of the various systems available, and offers practical information on the use of, and training to use, interactive whiteboards, as well as advice on their strategic management.

The future

Interactive technologies are here to stay and will continue to evolve. The current technology, which must employ a data projector and a touch-sensitive or matrix-type whiteboard, will probably give way to the fully interactive, wall-mounted, touch-sensitive plasma screen. Like a huge multimedia monitor it will act as a display and sound system for whatever computer is connected to it and be far more reliable than today's current offerings. But don't scrap that dry-wipe board just yet – or what will you use when the inevitable power failure occurs? It is sure to happen during your Ofsted inspection!

Chris Drage
Cisco Regional Academy Manager,
EiCAZ ICT support teacher,
ICT Journalist and author

About the author

Jenny Gage has worked for the Millennium Mathematics Project (www.mmp.maths.org) since 2001. Based in the Mathematics and Education Faculties of the University of Cambridge, the MMP works to help people see how exciting maths can be, and to provide a range of projects to help them enjoy maths. Jenny's role is to organise the Motivate videoconferencing project (www.motivate.maths.org), which provides videoconferences and accompanying project work for school students of all ages on a variety of mathematical and scientific topics. She also develops mathematical resources for the interactive whiteboard and gives courses for teachers on using an interactive whiteboard in the maths lesson.

Before working for the MMP, Jenny was a teacher for 15 years, teaching maths in schools in Derbyshire, Milton Keynes and Buckinghamshire. She also worked for the Open University for 15 years as a tutor on a number of maths courses. From 1998 until 2004, she carried out research for her PhD on how graphic calculators could help children in the 10–14 year age range to learn the basics of algebra.

When she isn't working, Jenny enjoys playing the piano, choral singing and going to concerts, and she always has at least one book on the go, often a thriller or a travel book. There is always time to read! She also enjoys exploring new places, both in the UK and abroad. Jenny is married with four grown-up children and two cats.

The Interactive Whiteboard CD-ROM

Minimum requirements to run the CD-ROM:

    PC only
    700 MHz
    64 Mb RAM
    CD-ROM
    Windows 98 SE, 2000, XP Home or Pro (SP1)
    Mouse or pointing device

In addition you will need Microsoft Office 2000 (or better). Smartboard or ACTIVprimary software to actually use the templates included.

If your CD does not start automatically after a few seconds, explore the CD and open the file "START.EXE".

Users who have the software Macromedia Flash MX studio or other Macromedia Flash authoring software may experience difficulty in opening ACTIVprimary work files when they click on the activity buttons of the CD-ROM. In some cases, the Macromedia software may attempt to (incorrectly) open the files.

This difficulty is due to both types of software using the same file extension (.FLP).

As a workaround the user may either:

   ⊙ Uninstall the Macromedia Flash software
   ⊙ Open the ACTIVprimary software and locate the following folders on the CD-ROM:

        MATHS_RESOURCES
        ENGLISH_RESOURCES
        OTHER_RESOURCES

The files can then be opened from within the ACTIVprimary software.

CD Resources

Resource Name	Type(s) of file in which it is available	Linked files (e.g. Excel, Dynamic Geometry)	Curriculum area	Features	Notes
Acids_alkalis	AS2, SMART, StarBoard		Science	Sorting activity	Properties of acids and alkalis, pH scale
Angle_ estimation	Excel		Maths	Uses random numbers, reveal answers by moving chart	Estimation of angles – various degrees of difficulty
Arciple	AS2, SMART, StarBoard, PowerPoint		Maths	Use of circle annotations to simplify a problem for generalisation	Problem adapted from one on nrich.maths.org
Arithmetic_ practice	Excel		Maths	Uses random numbers, reveal answers by changing font colour	Various degrees of difficulty
Circuit_symbols	AS2, SMART, StarBoard		Science	Use eraser tool to reveal hidden labels	
Coins_ Investigation	AS2, SMART, StarBoard, PowerPoint	Excel	Maths	Linked spreadsheet	How many ways can you make £1?
Das_Wetter	AS2, SMART, StarBoard, PowerPoint		MFL, German	Use of images to stimulate conversation	
Difference_two _squares	AS2, SMART, StarBoard, PowerPoint	Excel	Maths	Linked spreadsheet, images to reveal using eraser or animation	Looking at patterns, finding a formula and proving it
Directed_ number	Excel		Maths	Uses random numbers, reveal answers by changing font colour	Image of number line to facilitate

Resource Name	Type(s) of file in which it is available	Linked files (e.g. Excel, Dynamic Geometry)	Curriculum area	Features	Notes
Egyptian_arithmetic	PowerPoint		Maths		Egyptian division and fractions
Energy	AS2, SMART, StarBoard, PowerPoint		Science	Images to stimulate discussion	Advantages and disadvantages of energy sources
Factor_game	AS2, SMART, StarBoard, PowerPoint		Maths		Game – factors, primes
Finding_formulae	AS2, SMART, StarBoard, PowerPoint		Maths		Formulae from geometric patterns
Finding_information	AS2, SMART, StarBoard		English		Match question with source of information
Fractions_decimals_ratio	Excel		Maths	Uses IF formula to give feedback	Displays fractions and ratios as images, checks if equivalent
Graphs_background	AS2, SMART, StarBoard		Maths	Template	Blank sets of axes
Graphs_equations	AS2, SMART, StarBoard, PowerPoint		Maths		Graphs and equations to match
Graphs_template	Excel		Maths		Bar graphs, pie chart – display your own data
Handling_data	AS2, SMART, StarBoard, PowerPoint		Maths	Copy and paste from one page to another	Create/interpret a frequency polygon from data
Heart	AS2, SMART, StarBoard		Science	Hidden labels to reveal using eraser tool	Labelled heart diagram
Hot_cold_cubes	PowerPoint		Maths	Animations	Investigate addition/subtraction of directed numbers
Investigating_Fibonacci_numbers	AS2, SMART, StarBoard, PowerPoint	Excel	Maths	Linked spreadsheet	Investigate connection between Fibonacci numbers and Pythagorean triples
Investigating_quadratic_graphs	Excel		Maths	Use of sliders	Investigate how coefficients relate to shape of graph
La_Casa	PowerPoint		MFL, Italian	Images and text to stimulate conversation	
Magic_square	AS2, SMART, StarBoard, PowerPoint		Maths		Investigate a magic square with a difference – can lead to use of algebra

Resource Name	Type(s) of file in which it is available	Linked files (e.g. Excel, Dynamic Geometry)	Curriculum area	Features	Notes
Matching_ expressions	Starboard		Maths		Sort expressions into groups which are always the same
Parts_of_speech	AS2, PowerPoint		English	Hyperlinks between pages	Identify parts of speech – feedback given
Past_tense	AS2, SMART, StarBoard		MFL, French		Match parts of the past tense
Periodic_Table	Excel		Science	Use View>Full Screen	
Population_ statistics	AS2, SMART, StarBoard		Maths/Geo graphy	Copy and paste from one page to another	Create/interpret cumulative frequency graph of contrasting demographics
Pythagoras	AS2, SMART, StarBoard, PowerPoint	Geometers Sketchpad	Maths	Linked DG file	Demonstrate and prove Pythagoras' Th
Reflections.flp	AS2		Maths	Reflection in a horizontal/vertical axis	
Religions	AS2, SMART, StarBoard		RE	Images to promote discussion	
Roman_ Emperors	AS2, SMART, StarBoard, PowerPoint		History	Images to promote discussion	Create an obituary of a Roman Emperor
Squares	AS2, SMART, StarBoard		Maths		Strategy game – squares do not need to be horizontally based
Squares_ investigation	AS2, SMART, StarBoard, PowerPoint		Maths		Investigation of number of squares on a 'chess board'
Straight_line_ equations	Excel		Maths	Uses sliders	Gives feedback on equations of straight lines
Student_ Spanish	PowerPoint		MFL, Spanish	Linked sound files	Exemplar of using student work/sound files
Student1_ French	PowerPoint		MFL, French	Linked sound files	Exemplar of using student work/sound files
Student2_ French	PowerPoint		MFL, French	Linked sound files	Exemplar of using student work/sound files
Theories_ Universe	PowerPoint		History	Animations	Aristotelian and Copernican theories

Resource Name	Type(s) of file in which it is available	Linked files (e.g. Excel, Dynamic Geometry)	Curriculum area	Features	Notes
Think_of_a_number	AS2, SMART, StarBoard, PowerPoint		Maths	Reveal hidden answers/animations	Introduction to algebra
Today	AS2, SMART, StarBoard		MFL, French	Images and text to stimulate conversation	Use of past tenses
Tools	AS2, SMART, StarBoard		Technology	Images to stimulate discussion	
Tree_diagrams	PowerPoint		Maths	Animations	Setting up and using probability tree diagrams
UK_map1	AS2, SMART, StarBoard		Geography	Use eraser to reveal hidden labels	
UK_map2	AS2, SMART, StarBoard		Geography	Match areas on map with labels and photos	
Volcano	AS2, SMART, StarBoard, PowerPoint		Science	Creating a very basic resource	
W_Owen	Word		English	Use View>Full Screen – change background colour to reveal answers	Missing words
WWII	Starboard		History	Creating a very basic resource	Labelled map of fall of Europe in 1939–41

Interactive whiteboards: purchasing, installation and training

Chris Drage

Essentially, the aim here is to share suggestions, hints and tips that have been gleaned (sometimes painfully) from the past two years' experience of observing and using interactive whiteboards in both primary and secondary schools; the assumption being that although you, the teacher, may not be in the position to dictate what is or what is not purchased and installed in your classroom, you will at least be informed enough to know what you need, where and when. Often these matters arrive on the teacher's desk as a *fait accompli* and the teacher is the last person to find out. Often the teacher is 'consulted' beforehand but doesn't quite know what s/he is agreeing to. Armed with a bit of sound advice you should at least be able to influence the decision-making and steer the 'powers-that-be' into obtaining what you need, thus ending up with an excellent system that will serve you well for years to come.

The first question to be considered is: permanent or mobile? Permanent installation is, in my opinion, the only way to go. The SMART 2000i apart, trying to juggle the projector trolley, the IWB trolley and the laptop, and all the cables, can make you wonder if it is all worth it. Then dear Jenny goes and knocks it, and there goes the calibration again! Some large, mobile boards have wide 'feet' for stability but do not always fit comfortably through the non-standard classroom doors in our elderly buildings. I've seen too many potentially dangerous situations resulting from attempts to 'quickly' hook up a system ready for the session just after lunch. No – permanent installation is essential for ease of use and sustainability, unless you can afford the SMART 2000i which incorporates a rear projection unit (i.e. it has a computer and a projector mounted on its base) and can be handled with speed and safety.

Sighting the IWB is the next consideration. In many classrooms this may mean reorganising to a degree. After all, you want the students to have easy access to the IWB to ensure effective interactions with the software you are going to be using. Ideally, the students should also be able to see the IWB easily from their tables, but this is of secondary importance to having the board installed at a height where you and most of them are able to touch the top area. Can the IWB be installed low enough to the floor for diminutive Year 7 students to reach it? In my experience boards mounted too high do not get used for their true purpose and end up simply being very expensive projection screens. The balance between reachable height and being able to see from the back is most crucial. After that, it is a matter of ensuring that the place where the PC or laptop is to be placed has enough power sockets and that the cables are all properly trunked down the wall. A bit of planning at this stage will result in a system that works for you and your classroom organisation and, in turn, will boost your confidence by its presence. Don't let anyone discard your dry-wipe board. It is best fitted right next to the IWB. The technology will let you down at some stage.

One item frequently overlooked at the planning/purchasing stage is wall-mounted speakers. You cannot have an IWB fitted without speakers. You must be able to hear the sounds that accompany all those multimedia resources. From the modern languages to the maths department, having both sound and images in front of the class is one of the main reasons for putting an IWB in in the first place. Budget about £20–30 per board for these. Another item frequently overlooked is a video splitter to divide the signal from the back of the computer so that you can have the projector and the monitor (display) on concurrently. There are times when you don't want the class to be privy to what you are doing on the screen. Similarly, it is irksome to continually swap cables around every time you want to use the IWB.

Regarding installation, don't let the builders anywhere near and be wary of subcontractors. Bullet Point Presentations, Promethean, RM and Widewebs all understand schools' needs and undertake good installations. The best advice is to see what has worked well in other schools in your LEA and base your choice on that.

Before you finally go ahead and purchase the whole system ask about:

⊙ bulb warranty and replacement costs – most projectors come today with a three-year bulb warranty. LCD projector bulbs typically cost between £200 and £350;

⊙ the life of the batteries in the pens (with some boards) – this may seem a minor consideration but it will become part of an enduring running cost;

⊙ the cost of a replacement pen/stylus (currently, 2005, £40 (Promethean) and £42.80 (RM));

⊙ Does the IWB membrane have a 'life' – does the pen or stylus have one too?

⊙ How resistant is it to knocks and scratches?

⊙ How much training does the vendor offer, or is it all down to the overworked ICT co-ordinator?

⊙ Who is going to take responsibility for technical support from within the school?

Some schools opted to just have projectors installed and to use the dry-wipe board or a bespoke projector screen for the display. If your classroom is one of these and your school now has the funding to purchase IWBs to go with them, ensure that the decision-makers measure the 'image throw' (projection) of your existing mounted projector to ensure that it will fill the proposed IWB surface. Overlooking this can prove expensive if your projector needs to be moved with its ceiling mount.

Which type of IWB system should you purchase? Most schools I visit seem to have fitted either SMARTBoards (SMART Technologies), Promethean Boards (Promethean), Class Boards (RM) or Cambridge Boards (Cambridge-Hitachi), and occasionally a mixture of all four. This is no accident as these four companies do not just provide the hardware and basic software but have also concentrated their efforts on providing a range of tools and curriculum-related software that is often a school's sole reason for choosing a particular make of IWB. All of them are constantly making improvements and enhancements to their software. However, should your department find itself with a range of different boards and IWB software which is proving difficult to master, due to having a variety of systems, then you may wish to opt for an IWB 'toolkit' that works with every system: RM's Easiteach Studio. By opting for a single IWB toolkit, time spent on familiarisation and training is more efficiently spent.

Post-installation

The IWB is in place and now you are expected to use all this brand-new equipment. The least you can expect is a one-hour, hands-on training session. Training is not only necessary for staff but also paramount, as this technology demands a few new and different teaching techniques. Experience shows that the only way to get to grips with the new *modus operandi* is to take things forward slowly and comfortably. If you lack confidence then just use it as a simple screen for a few weeks and practise with some of the basic tools when the pupils are absent. One golden health & safety rule to remember is: if you can see your own shadow on the board don't turn to look at the class! The 'blast' of light from the projector can cause much discomfort and, as yet, we are not fully aware of the effects of working for long periods under such intense, directional light.

In practice

One thing has become blindingly clear: using an IWB does not make a good teacher; it cannot make a poor teacher any better; but in the hands of a skilled and practised teacher it can take teaching and learning to new heights. For example, I saw a teacher introducing Shakespeare to lower ability Year 7s using her projector (she had no access to an IWB) to great effect in order to reduce the amount of text in front of her students. She had a pull-down screen in front of her dry-wipe board. By using the zoom feature on her remote handset she was able to enlarge the key bit of text she wanted them to focus on, and when it came to the point where she wanted to highlight all the proper nouns and certain other key words she simply pulled up the screen, got her dry marker and did all the annotations on the projected image on the whiteboard. When she had completed that part, she simply pulled down the screen, reset the zoom and moved to her next slide. She certainly could have made use of an IWB!

Five basic steps in gaining competence with an interactive whiteboard

1. Become completely familiar with the curriculum software you intend to use on the IWB in front of the class. The last thing a less-than-confident teacher needs is uncertainty about how to 'drive' the software they are using.

2. Become practised and confident in whole-class teaching.

3. Become used to using the basic tools included with your IWB. Try annotating, highlighting, using the 'spotlight' and 'blind'. Gradually extend your repertoire to include the more sophisticated tools.

4. Ensure that the IWB software tools like the SMART Notebook or Cambridge-Hitachi's Flipchart are on your teacher's laptop so that you can work on your skills away from the classroom.

5. Practise, practise, practise – it is the only way you are going to be a teacher in control of the technology driving teaching and learning in the twenty-first century.

Introduction

'It's brilliant. I wouldn't want to go back to lessons without it.'

(Y8 student)

'It's fun, it looks a bit better, more neat. I can understand the handwriting. And it's cool 'cos you get to have a go on it.'

(Y7 student)

'It's good because you can see what's happening – much better than diagrams.'

(Y8 student)

'It's really good, a really useful classroom tool. You can do more demonstrations, have more fun, more colour, more pictures – the whole class can join in.'

(Science teacher)

'I wouldn't want to go back to doing without an IWB. I'm used to teaching through it. It's useful to be able to use texts, to annotate, to switch between one thing and another, to use images and film, to be able to revisit things.'

(English teacher)

'It's really cool for playing movies, educational games. I've used it for a few years now – we had them at my primary school as well. No, the novelty hasn't worn off yet – there's lots more I don't know.'

(Y8 student)

'It's great because the teacher can prepare the lesson and go through things really quickly, but when it breaks down it's a problem because it's so good when it works.'

(Y10 student)

'I couldn't teach without it. When it didn't work one time, it was awful!'

(Maths teacher)

'It's very useful. Sometimes it's much more worthwhile than others, especially in science, maths and English. In English, people can have discussions and bring them back, watch films and images. In science, you can have links to websites, and have things ready prepared.'

(Y10 student)

'It's pretty good. You can do loads of stuff much better than just writing on a normal whiteboard. You can play games and move things around and it's easier to see. We get more done than in subjects that don't have it.'

(Y7 student)

While I was writing this book I interviewed a number of teachers and observed many lessons in secondary schools, finding out how interactive whiteboards are used in the classroom, and about teachers' and students' attitudes to them. I heard comments like those above over and over again.

Interactive whiteboards are rapidly entering our classrooms, and many teachers are excited by this new technology. They look forward to finding out what they can do with it and how it can be used to enhance their teaching. Even experienced users say they have yet to use anything like the full potential of the board. Others wonder if they will ever get the hang of using it, fearing it will let them down at a crucial moment. There are also those who feel that it has nothing to offer that they cannot achieve in other ways.

An IWB is a tool which, when used well, will help a teacher to teach well. However, a poor lesson will remain exactly that if the IWB is used in a way that is unsuitable and irrelevant. In the hands of a good teacher, an IWB can make lessons exciting, interactive and well-paced, motivating the students and providing them with experiences they remember. An IWB can be used to support good lessons, full of interest, with well-thought-out content and authentic tasks. Equally, it can be used to support inappropriate lesson content and style, providing an excuse for tedious, one-way lessons that are only remembered because they are so boring.

Although an IWB is called 'interactive', interaction is not really to do with the board; it is between the students, the teacher and the subject content of the lesson which may be displayed on the board. It is not the board which determines how much interaction occurs, but the teacher using it. Effective use of an IWB should encourage both teachers and students to ask deeper, more probing questions and to search for answers together. An IWB can provide a focus for students to contribute their ideas, and to listen to those of others. It can also lead to greater incorporation of ICT, so that ICT is integrated into the curriculum, rather than seen as something separate that is only encountered in the ICT suite.

The purpose of this book is to help teachers to use an IWB in a way that supports effective practice and enhances learning. It is intended both for teachers who have little or no experience of using an IWB, and for those who feel that they have made a start, but would like to find out more about what it can do to support their teaching.

With this book, there is a CD of classroom resources to be used with an IWB. These do not attempt to provide a full set of teaching materials for the IWB – to do this across many curriculum areas would be a huge undertaking. Many resources can now be found, free of charge, on the internet, and some suggestions of websites are given at the end of the book. Commercially available resources can also be used to provide content for the IWB. What I hope the resources on the CD will do is to help teachers to explore what they can do with their IWBs: these resources are starting points to enable teachers to create their own lesson materials. To facilitate this, the resources are not described in this book by subject content but by the techniques they use.

Detailed instructions are given for the use of commonly available software such as Microsoft Word, Excel and Paint, and presentation software such as Microsoft PowerPoint and the software that comes with the IWB. There are a number of makes of board available, and it has not been possible to provide specific instructions for all of them. I have focused on the SMARTBoard, Promethean's ACTIVstudio2 software and the Hitachi StarBoard. I hope that teachers with other boards will nevertheless find much that is helpful to them, and that with their own User's Guide to help them they will be able to make use of the ideas in this book.

Resources on the CD are in Microsoft Word, Excel and PowerPoint (XP versions, 2003), SMARTBoard software (version 9.0, 2005), ACTIVstudio2 software (version 1.0.3, 2004), Hitachi StarBoard software (version 6.12, 2004) and Geometer's Sketchpad (version 4.05). The resources should also open in some earlier versions of the relevant software. Up-to-date versions of IWB software can usually be downloaded from the internet or bought for a small additional amount (see Appendix 1 for website addresses).

This book is divided into two parts. Part 1 covers practical and pedagogical issues. In Chapter 1, basic practical matters are considered, such as what can the IWB do, what types are there and where should they be put? The question of how an IWB can enhance teaching and learning in secondary school teaching is discussed in Chapter 2: Does it take up a lot of time to prepare materials for it? Does it help integrate ICT into the curriculum? In Chapter 3, the pedagogy of teaching with an IWB is discussed: How is an IWB best used in the classroom? How does its use affect teaching and learning? Is it only for use with the whole class? How does its use affect different types of learners? What about students with special educational needs?

Part 2 is a 'how to' guide to preparing lesson content. In Chapter 4, the functionality of an IWB is described, together with suggestions for getting started. Instructions are given for common operations in various different applications, such as printing and saving, using the annotation tools, creating templates and worksheets and using presentation software. Chapter 5 then gives a detailed overview of Word, PowerPoint, Excel and Paint, while Chapter 6 does the same for ACTIVstudio2 software, SMARTBoard software and Hitachi StarBoard software. Finally, Chapter 7 describes useful techniques which can be used in creating lesson resources, illustrated from those available on the CD.

It is my belief that the interactive whiteboard has the ability to transform our classrooms, bringing action, colour and variety to teaching and learning. All the students I observed were very enthusiastic about its impact on their lessons, and the teachers who were already using the IWB were excited by the possibilities. I hope that this book will help others to explore for themselves the potential of the interactive whiteboard.

Getting started

Ten things you should find out about your IWB sooner rather than later

1. How to save work in progress for later.

2. How to use the IWB annotation tools over any document or web page.

3. How to print out pages from the IWB for your students.

4. Where to find backgrounds, such as specialist paper, grids, graph paper, music paper etc.

5. How to use the ScreenCapture/Camera tool.

6. How to use the Handwriting Recognition tool.

7. How to add images to documents.

8. How to add sounds to documents.

9. How to create links to all the resources – such as web pages, other documents, pictures, video, sound – that you want to use during a lesson.

10. How to create a presentation in PowerPoint and with the IWB software.

Ten tips to help you use your IWB more effectively

1. The most important interactions are between the students and the teacher and between the students and the lesson content, not between the teacher and the IWB.

2. Give students frequent access to the board.

3. Share resources with colleagues in your own department/school and more widely if appropriate.

4. Create an effective departmental filing system for resources – everyone needs to know where to find what they want and what every resource contains.

5. Have an internet connection to the IWB.

6. Connect the IWB to the school network so that students' work can be displayed easily and quickly.

7. Have a scanner available with the IWB so that hand-produced work can be easily and quickly displayed.

8. Keep a digital camera with you so that you can capture images for immediate or future use.

9. Always have an alternative strategy in case of a technical problem. If the IWB isn't working, try re-opening the software. If that doesn't work, try restarting the computer. If that doesn't work, move to your alternative strategy.

10. Don't take away the ordinary whiteboard. (What happens if the IWB breaks down?)

Ten things to avoid

1. Using the IWB as an excuse for too much teacher talk and not enough student involvement. (It isn't the board that needs to be interactive!)

2. Making your presentations say everything there is to say about a topic with no room for discussion and student input.

3. Using flashy technical effects that do not add to the students' understanding.

4. Being intimidated by the IWB.

5. Using the IWB only for handwritten notes – why do you need an IWB for that?

6. Being afraid to experiment with new ways of presenting topics.

7. Being afraid to try out new ways of using what the IWB can offer.

8. Filling page after page with text.

9. Using the IWB as a textbook on the wall – students need to interact with the material.

10. Thinking you've ever learnt everything there is to know about using the IWB to enhance your teaching.

PART 1

The Interactive Whiteboard in the Classroom

What is an interactive whiteboard? It is essentially a large computer screen which is sensitive to touch. To operate an IWB you need a computer and a data projector in addition to the board itself. The content of the computer screen is displayed on the board using the data projector, and the computer can then be operated either from the computer mouse and keyboard or directly from the whiteboard. With some boards you can use your finger to write and draw on them and to operate software; other boards require special pens (equivalent to the mouse on a conventional computer).

An IWB can be used to replace the ordinary whiteboard and the overhead projector. In addition, it can be used to demonstrate and annotate web resources or any computer application or file on the school computer network. IWBs can also be used with video, music and picture files. If there is a scanner available, or if students are working at networked computers, their work can be displayed to the rest of the class on the IWB and saved as a record of their progress. In fact, anything displayed on the board, including annotations, can be saved for later and/or printed.

IWB use can support the incorporation of other ICT into lessons by:

◉ providing access to a wide range of computer software and programs without the need to go to a computer suite;

◉ providing a focus for the students' attention;

◉ providing a large display;

◉ encouraging discussion about issues other than technical problems.

The IWB is an excellent way of integrating ICT into lessons in a way that does not lead to the teacher feeling redundant, deskilled or exhausted. The role of the teacher is central to effective classroom practice, but unfortunately, all too often ICT use can make teachers feel either that the students know more than they do, or that their role is reduced to rushing around sorting out technical problems. With an IWB you remain in control of what happens and what is discussed, so that important educational points can be focused on rather than lost in the technicalities. You can demonstrate new ICT applications to the students so that they can see what is expected of them, and what they should achieve. You can choose when to intervene to focus all the students on one particular issue. If the students are working at individual computers, they can turn to look at the IWB to facilitate discussion of a problem or to draw attention to something, then return to their own monitors.

However, IWB use is not simply about incorporating more ICT in lessons. As we shall see, the IWB can provide a dynamic approach to teaching and learning resources that has the potential to revolutionise our classrooms.

CHAPTER 1

The practicalities

What is an interactive whiteboard?

An IWB can be thought of as a mix of a computer, an overhead projector and a white-board (or chalkboard).

The interactive whiteboard as a computer

An IWB is run by a computer, and the whiteboard display is exactly the same as the display on the computer monitor. The board acts as an extra computer screen but with the additional property of being interactive. Some interactive white-boards have special pens that act like a computer mouse, while others can be operated with a finger (although a wet or sticky finger will not work). Boards which can be operated directly with a finger may also have special pens.

Any software or files that are available on the computer can be accessed using the pen/finger and used on the IWB. This can be done either through the computer keyboard or directly on the board by clicking or tapping with the pen/finger. Boards can also be operated with a wireless mouse/keyboard. The board will probably also have its own on-screen keyboard so that text can be typed directly without having to use the computer keyboard. If it does not, there is an on-screen keyboard in Windows XP, which is accessed from the Start button. To operate the on-screen keyboard you just tap your finger or the pen on the keys required.

> **start**
>
> All programs>
> Access>
> Accessibility>
> On-screen
> keyboard

An IWB also allows you to use the internet interactively, with the pen/finger used to work directly at the board. This is particularly useful for displaying and working with a site with a whole class: the page can be clearly seen by all the students at the same time so that they are all focused on the same thing.

The interactive whiteboard as an overhead projector

Teachers who have used OHPs in the past will have banks of transparencies that they will want to be able to continue to use. Provided there is a scanner available, any worksheet or transparency can be scanned into the computer so that it is then accessible on the IWB. The IWB has annotation tools that allow a document to be written on, highlighted and drawn on: the document can be annotated in the same way as an OHP transparency. The contents of the document can also be revealed bit by bit, as with an OHP – most IWB software contains a screen that can be removed gradually.

The advantage the IWB has over an ordinary OHP is that everything can be saved for another time, including both original documents and annotated documents. Either can also be printed if desired. Unlike overhead transparencies, these files will not be lost or become messy. They are always there, on the computer system, as good as new.

The interactive whiteboard as a whiteboard/chalkboard

As its name suggests, an IWB is also a whiteboard or chalkboard which has its own software. On a SMARTBoard this is called a notebook; in ACTIVstudio2 and on the Hitachi StarBoard it is known as a flipchart. The IWB notebook or flipchart has many clean pages ready for use – far more than anyone could ever use in a lesson or a whole series of lessons. One click or tap on the appropriate icon will bring up a clean page whenever it is needed. However, the previous pages will still be available to be returned to as appropriate. All the pages used can be displayed to allow easy navigation between them, or so that their order can be changed.

Unlike a conventional whiteboard, you can change the background colour to anything you like in order to add emphasis or interest to a page. Light reflected from a whiteboard can sometimes prevent some students from seeing properly. You can avoid this by choosing a different colour. Many other backgrounds are also available in the IWB software, including lines, square grids, graph paper, musical staves and maps.

Different types of IWBs

There are two main types of IWB available. One type has a sensitive board surface, which may mean you can use your finger to write on the board or to change from one program to another. A well-known make of board with a sensitive surface, which can be operated using just a finger, is the SMARTBoard. SMARTBoards also have a tray containing pens which write like ordinary whiteboard pens (although they do not use real ink). In addition, there are several websites where lesson plans, classroom resources and case studies can be downloaded. (See Appendix 1 for further information about websites.) The SMARTBoard software includes clipart and specialist images, and concept-mapping software.

The second main type of IWB has a surface that is not touch-sensitive and which needs a special mouse pen. The electronics are inside the board, which makes this type of board less likely to be damaged, since their surfaces can take a reasonable degree of normal wear and tear. Well-known makes include the Promethean ACTIVboard and the Hitachi StarBoard. Both these manufacturers have specifically designed their boards and software with an educational focus. The StarBoard's software includes lesson content for maths and science, and content for other curriculum areas can be purchased separately. ACTIVstudio2 software contains lesson content for all curriculum areas. Further information and materials can be found on both the Promethean and Cambridge-Hitachi websites (Appendix 1). Both the StarBoard and ACTIVstudio2 also provide a range of specialist mathematical tools, and the facility to reflect objects as well as rotate them.

For some types of board, slates or tablets which can be used by students at their own tables or anywhere else in the room are also available. Another facility offered by some manufacturers is a 'voting system'. Students give their responses to questions using a hand-held voting keypad which uses wireless communication. Questions can be shown on the IWB together with various choices for the answer. Each student's response is recorded, so that a record can be kept of both class performance on the questions and each person's individual performance. Alternatively, students' choices can be anonymised so that sensitive questions, such as a survey of smoking habits, can be asked without the risk of the teacher knowing which student gave which answer.

Fixed or mobile?

Most makes of board give the option of having them fixed to the wall or free-mounted on their own stand. Both have advantages and disadvantages. A wall-mounted board is less vulnerable to damage; it is also less likely to be knocked during a lesson so that it needs recalibrating. However, once a board is mounted on the wall and the data projector on the ceiling, it is more or less permanently fixed. A board on a wheeled stand together with an unmounted data projector can be used in different rooms, which provides much greater flexibility of use.

The needs of all the students and the teacher should be considered in deciding whether to go for fixed boards or not. It is important that every child has a clear view of the board and can easily reach it. If the room does not have blinds, the board needs to be sited so that it is not in direct sunlight as this will mean that it is difficult to see anything except the glare of reflected light. An adequate data projector is also important if students are to see what is on the board clearly, so check the resolution of the projector if you need to be able to show fine detail on your IWB. Whether the board is fixed or mobile, there needs to be enough room around it for the teacher or students to stand at either side without casting a shadow on the board.

Experience seems to indicate that a fixed board in a teacher's own classroom will be used regularly and frequently. Access to the board is not a problem and you have the opportunity to get used to using it, and do not need to spend precious time setting up the board or the projector. If the board and projector are not permanently set up, a good 15 minutes can be lost at the beginning of the day or the lesson getting this done. If this is the case, teachers are much less likely to use the board on a regular basis, and so are less likely to become effective users.

There needs to be a PC or laptop sited near the board, and the positioning of this also needs careful consideration: both ease of use and safety need to be considered. To gain the full benefit of the IWB, the PC or laptop should be connected to the school computer network and to the internet. If it is networked, then work done by students at their own computers can easily be displayed and resources can be shared by all the staff. However, speed of logging on to the school network may be a problem when you are not teaching in your own room.

You need also to consider technical problems, as they may mean that a planned lesson cannot proceed, particularly if you lack experience with IWBs. This could be due to network or equipment failure, or simply to use by an inexperienced person. This is not to say that an inexperienced teacher is more likely to have things go wrong, but that they may have less idea of how to remedy a problem. Whatever the cause, you need to have an alternative strategy you can use if the board refuses to co-operate and cannot be fixed speedily. Often, rebooting the computer and/or restarting the software helps. If this does not sort out the problem, it is better to do something else than to keep everyone waiting.

In some classrooms, when an IWB is installed the ordinary whiteboard is removed. This is a mistake, as the ordinary whiteboard will continue to be useful, if only for the occasions when the IWB is out of action for some reason. A teacher unfamiliar with the operation of the IWB using the room will appreciate the continued presence of an ordinary whiteboard, and it can also be useful for putting up quick messages for the students. There are also occasions when you just want a lot of white space, and having the ordinary board available as well as the IWB enables you to display more material at once.

Cheaper alternatives to an IWB

Some schools decide to start with just a data projector, rather than the more expensive IWB. Resources can be prepared in advance on the computer and the data projector used to display the computer screen onto any suitable surface. If the image is projected onto an ordinary whiteboard it can also be annotated, so that some of the advantages of the IWB are available. PowerPoint presentations can also be annotated using the mouse. However, annotations cannot be saved as they could with an IWB, and the whiteboard surface is not interactive. This means all changes need to be made at the computer keyboard, and some of the dynamic qualities of an IWB are not available.

There are teachers who are unconvinced by the claims of the IWB, claiming that using a data projector alone gives them all the functionality they need. With a data projector and a computer, you can access the internet and any software application available in school. However, the IWB does offer significantly more than a data projector and computer – annotations can be saved and printed out; images can be made dynamic so that they can be moved across the page, changed in colour or size, or animated, quickly and easily.

For a minority of teachers the data projector alone seems sufficient as they rarely use the IWB software and can annotate directly onto an ordinary whiteboard surface if necessary. However, it is the interaction that is important.

Using an IWB presents significant advantages in terms of interactivity – you can present a topic at the board while maintaining a dynamic relationship with the class, or you can choose to have students up to interact with the lesson material. Some of these advantages are also available with just a data projector, but direct interaction with the content is not.

> 'It wouldn't be enough for me, but it is for a lot of other people. I like having the pupils up there – it speeds up the lesson, focuses the students on me and the board, because of the immediacy of it. Other teachers in my school are progressing onto the IWB from the projector. You can book the data projector, use it to show you need an IWB.'

Sometimes cost will dictate what equipment is available. Putting a data projector and a computer in the classroom will enable teachers to start using more resources and more ICT in their lessons. If at some later point an IWB can also be provided, these teachers will be well on the way to using it effectively. Where possible, the flipcharts and notebooks on the CD accompanying this book have been prepared in PowerPoint as well as IWB software, so that they can be used with just a data projector and a computer.

Another option is to convert an ordinary whiteboard to an electronic board. This requires software – for example that marketed by Mimio – which allows the movement of ordinary dry-marker pens to be tracked using ultrasound and then converted to a computer file, so that the content of the board can be saved, printed out and used again as desired. Anything written or drawn on an existing whiteboard can be captured and edited, and all other applications can be annotated using the special mouse pen. Objects can then be moved, re-sized and rotated. In addition, the latest version of Mimio software contains lesson resources and software for the creation of materials, together with backgrounds and clipart. The software is available as a free download (see Appendix 1 for details), although it is necessary to buy the physical equipment needed to convert what is written on the whiteboard to an electronic form. Such systems have the advantage of being light, portable and inexpensive as they can be used with existing conventional whiteboards and there is no need for a PC to be located in the classroom.

CHAPTER 2

How can an interactive whiteboard enhance teaching and learning in the secondary school?

There are now many case studies describing IWB use on the internet. Advocates of the IWB suggest that its use:

◉ helps teachers to structure their lessons;

◉ enables ICT use to be more integrated into lessons;

◉ supports collaborative learning;

◉ can help develop students' cognitive skills;

◉ helps to attract and retain students' attention;

◉ saves time taken up in note-taking or scribing;

◉ can provide large, attractive text and images;

◉ allows text and images to be moved around the board and/or changed;

◉ provides additional software which includes a variety of additional graphics, such as maps, specialist backgrounds and a wide range of images; and

◉ allows work to be saved or printed out.

Some research has suggested that high IWB use leads to more questioning – both of students and by them – more stimulating discussion and better explanations. Students enjoy the additional variety which IWB use allows. Many different resources can be used in a lesson, and these can be returned to whenever necessary. Moving frequently between resources helps students to refocus their attention if they are distracted, helping them to stay on task longer. Students benefit from being able to touch the board and physically move objects around it. Using audio and video files allows voices from outside the classroom to be heard, again refocusing attention. All learners can benefit from the increased opportunities for more auditory learning, more visual learning and more kinaesthetic learning.

In the lessons I observed while I was researching this book, it was very apparent that students found it easier to stay on task when the IWB was used. For instance, a group of mixed-ability Year 8 students kept a whole-class discussion on images from the film *Batman* going for well over half an hour because they were so interested in the exchange. The quality of the discussion is shown in this excerpt:

T: What I love about doing this is that people always come up with new stuff! [annotating an image to demonstrate a point made by a girl].

S: Oh, my goodness! That's so cool!

[Many students have their hands up at this point, desperate to contribute their ideas.]

T: What difference does it make that he's looking up?

[A quick discussion between students and the teacher follows, covering ideas that his parents are in heaven and he's looking up to them; that things up high are ideal or unreal.]

S: They've got more status than him. They're in the light. They're all smiling and happy.

T: If they're dead, how can they have power?

S: Because it's in his mind. Because they're higher up and they were, like, his parents – he wants to live up to them.

T: How is his unhappiness suggested in the picture?

S: The room is dark and empty. There are shadows and echoes. The ceiling is high and the fireplace is black. That is hell and they're on top of it. [There is a picture of the parents above the fireplace.]

S: It's a long shot, so he looks small.

T: What do you think the empty room represents?

S: It's dark, he feels lonely.

S: The empty room represents his empty heart.

[At this point, the teacher tried to cut the discussion short, but the students would not let him.]

S: The room represents his life, it's empty. The fire says there's no spark, no real things happening in his life. He's done no real good except for his Batman things.

And so the discussion continued, with all the students vying with each other to present their point of view. The images from the film on the IWB provided the focus for the discussion, which the teacher annotated, forming a record that allowed both the students and the teacher to refer back to previous points. There was no loss of pace while he started and stopped the video, he could return to an earlier frame instantly and he could directly annotate the video – he had complete control of the lesson at all times. I came out of this lesson feeling tremendously excited both by the quality of the discussion and the potential of the IWB to provide the focus and stimulation for it.

Access

Access to an IWB on a regular basis is crucial if teachers are to integrate it into their lessons. If teachers do not have reliable access to a board it is very unlikely that they will move beyond using the board in a very basic way. There is also a risk that the board is used 'because it's my turn', rather than because it is an effective and appropriate means of delivering the planned lesson. If a board is not always available, teachers need to be sure that if they spend time preparing a lesson using the IWB they will actually be able to use it on the day.

It is an advantage for you to have a laptop, so that you can prepare IWB materials at home and discover the board's potential at your own pace. An alternative would be to make the software available for teachers to install on their home computers. Files can then be brought into school on a floppy disk or CD or sent in as an e-mail attachment. Becoming proficient in using the IWB requires time and the opportunity for private exploration in an unpressurised atmosphere that allows teachers to think creatively.

Training

It is quite possible to use an IWB like an ordinary whiteboard (although possibly using special pens) and never make any use of its functionality. This may happen if teachers do not currently use ICT much and are given no training in the use of the IWB. But what an expensive whiteboard it then becomes! It is important that teachers have the time and help they need to become confident in their use of the IWB so that they do not stick with just a few basic operations. There will, however, be occasions when use of the IWB is restricted to simply using it as a whiteboard, because that is what is appropriate. There is no reason why you should feel you have to do something innovative or creative with it in every lesson.

The IWB screen is a Windows environment, like any other computer likely to be found in a school, so you need to be familiar with this program and know how to access and manipulate the software and files on the system you have in your school. Once you are used to how Windows operates, and basic word processing, then using the IWB should not be a problem. If you are new to the IWB, it makes sense to start with an application you are already accustomed to using, so that you can learn how to use the board with a familiar activity. There is a learning curve to be followed in finding out all that it can do, but there is no reason why this should not be a gradual learning curve which you follow at the pace that suits you. If you are worried about your keyboard or mouse skills, you will find that these improve rapidly with practice.

I asked the teachers I interviewed how long they felt it had taken them to become competent with the IWB. Answers ranged from a couple of weeks to a couple of months to 'six months to be really fluent'. This was a typical response:

> I still don't think I'm competent – it's an ongoing process. You can reach a basic level of competence in about a couple of hours. Then you . . . broaden your perspectives about how you can use the capabilities of the technology more effectively.

The consensus was that you can get going, enough to be able to run a lesson perfectly satisfactorily, in a couple of weeks, but that there would always be opportunities to explore further how the board can be used to provide effective teaching resources.

Teachers who already use a word processor, specialist software or the internet with their classes will have a head start over those who use ICT very little, but there is no reason why even the least ICT-literate teacher should not feel confident about using the board with practice and with support from colleagues. To progress beyond previous ICT use you will need to become familiar with the software which comes with the IWB. IWBs have annotation tools (pens, highlighters, erasers etc.) which can be used with any other application – such as Word, PowerPoint or a spreadsheet – to write notes, highlight text, draw arrows to particular items etc. These tools also contain a 'camera' that can be used to take a snapshot of any part of the screen. In addition to the annotation tools, which can be used with any application or the internet, IWBs also provide notebooks or flipcharts which you can use to produce your own interactive, dynamic presentations. Using the annotation tools and notebooks/flipcharts is discussed in more detail in Part 2.

Many teachers emphasised how much it helps to have a colleague or two with whom to share ideas and problems:

> If somebody knows how to do something they should share it . . . Anyone can always observe my lessons, or have a go in a one-to-one demo. I'll always go in and help others if I'm available.

Using an IWB provides teachers with opportunities to learn from each other through using each other's resources. It also enables teachers to develop their own practice through sharing ideas and techniques.

Learning how to use an IWB effectively can be speeded up by training courses provided by the LEA or by independent trainers, or by getting someone from the company selling the board to come and demonstrate how the board works and how to start using it. However, if teachers cannot follow up their training by using the board regularly, they will soon forget what they have been taught and will need to spend time going over the training again.

Finally, whatever the training provided, time needs to be put aside for teachers to practise before using the board in front of the class, and for them to prepare classroom resources.

Lesson preparation

Inevitably, starting to use an IWB to create lesson materials will add to preparation time, but this should decrease again once you have familiarised yourself with how it functions. The best way to reduce preparation time in the long term, however, is to share resources with colleagues, so that a bank of lesson resources can be built up for everyone to use. Pairing a novice with a more experienced user will also help, particularly if they can team teach with the IWB from time to time. One teacher commented that the staff at her school had been very nervous when computers were introduced a few years earlier, but that IWB introduction was going better: 'They see it, then decide they want it, then there's on-the-spot help available'.

Any increased preparation time is likely to mean that a lesson is better prepared. Furthermore, having everything ready on the IWB means that you can spend more time during the lesson working directly with the students. Continuing a topic begun earlier just requires opening up the file – there is no need to write things up again. Complicated diagrams or maps can be prepared perfectly in advance – no need for sketches that require a leap of the imagination from the students.

Using an IWB does not mean that you will need to spend a lot more time on preparation indefinitely, however. Lessons can be given extra impact using the internet, which just requires saving appropriate websites in 'Favourites'. Resources do not always need to be prepared from scratch, but, once created, can be revised for future use. Sharing standard lessons in a department removes the need to do everything yourself, and gives new teachers a starting point using lessons already prepared by more experienced colleagues.

For some teachers, increased preparation results from doing things they would not have done before, such as animations and interactive activities. Creating a big flipchart/notebook with differentiated paths through it for different groups of students is time-consuming, as is preparing whole topics at a variety of levels. However, sharing such major projects and re-using them in future years can reduce future workload, and is likely to be a major contribution to good practice throughout a department. If the IWB can help teachers share more resources and work together to produce high-quality lessons, then it will provide a valuable service.

Of course, just because an IWB is available does not mean that it has to be used all the time. One aspect of good preparation is choosing the best tool for the job, and there will be times when the IWB is not the best way to present a topic, or when students need to work with practical materials. Neither does every lesson require brand-new resources. The lessons in which to start incorporating IWB use are probably not those that are already very good ones. If you have a lesson that scores nine out of ten, why mess with it? However, if you have a lesson that you would only score six out of ten, then that might be a good one in which to plan using the IWB.

Professional presentation

Of necessity, the display on an ordinary whiteboard is static and impermanent, and can only consist of anything that can be drawn on it, written on it or stuck to it. The IWB display, however, can be permanent, always available and always in perfect condition. Such displays can be dynamic and can call up a host of resources from the school network and the web. Teachers and students using an IWB can easily achieve a level of presentation that matches professionally designed resources, unlike much that is drawn or written on an ordinary board.

This is particularly useful in areas of the curriculum where visual resources are important, such as art, geography, mathematics, MFL and science. In one science lesson I observed, a Year 8 mixed-ability group was shown a picture of volunteers in New York giving blood in the immediate aftermath of the events of 11 September 2001. The class was spellbound. That photo, together with the knowledge that almost none of the blood was needed that day, impacted deeply on the students. The teacher also showed them photos of red and white blood cells, and a diagram and photo of the heart. The visual content of this lesson stimulated good questions from the students and enabled the teacher to pose several thought-provoking questions of her own.

With an IWB, a teacher can produce a map, correct in every detail, virtually instantaneously. The map can be written across, have places marked on it, have special features drawn on it and be saved for another occasion. The original is also available for another time, still in perfect condition. Diagrams and graphs in maths lessons can be drawn in advance, providing perfect exemplars for the students at the click of a pen. The MFL lesson can be enlivened with photos or clipart for the class to describe, providing a vehicle for the introduction of vocabulary and for all kinds of oral work.

Video, diagrams and images that are large, clear, in colour and dynamic make it easier for students to understand complex concepts and to remember them. Video clips can be stopped at any point, annotated using the IWB annotation tools and then started again. In some types of IWB software, the image with its annotations can be saved and made part of notes printed out for the students.

Support for curriculum areas

IWB software has many resources and tools that can be used to support curriculum areas. These range from having calculator, protractor and ruler tools, to being able to access presentations on radioactive decay, say, or chemical limestone weathering, or the alphabet in Spanish. Images such as maps and geographical features, scientific equipment, musical instruments and notes, and much more, are available to illustrate lesson materials. Further resources can be downloaded from a wide range of websites, including the manufacturers', DfES's, LEAs', other schools', and many others (see Appendix 1 for further details).

Backgrounds available in IWB software include square grids, graph paper, music paper and a variety of maps. Being able to use squared or graph paper and really straight lines means that graphs are correctly drawn, and students no longer have to use their imaginations to work out what they should look like. Some IWB software also includes music and other sounds.

Integrating ICT into lessons

Proponents of ICT use in the classroom claim many benefits for its use, including increased interactivity, provisionality, access to information and the speeding up of routine tasks.

For many students, the interactivity and provisionality of ICT use decreases their fear of public exposure. If something is incorrect it can be quickly deleted and another answer substituted. This means that many different ideas can be tried out without loss of face. This is particularly helpful for less confident students and those who find writing difficult.

We have access to more information today than ever before, and the amount of information 'out there' is growing all the time. It is therefore increasingly important that students learn how to use the internet safely and appropriately. They need to know how to search effectively for information and how to evaluate what they find, realising that sites vary considerably in the quality of the information they provide.

Using ICT, tasks such as collecting and displaying data can be completed quickly and effectively with appropriate software; calculations can be carried out and results displayed using presentation software. Time saved on these tasks can be used to help students develop higher-order skills, such as deciding what are good questions to research, what aspects of data should be displayed, whether there is bias in the questions or data, and so on.

Unfortunately, there have been occasions where teachers have interpreted their role when ICT is used as that of facilitating the students' interactions with the software and managing the classroom. Of course, these are important, but it is also necessary for the teacher to continue to support the students' learning by asking questions, probing to see how well they understand. The IWB can help this to occur by providing a focus for discussion. Where computers are networked, any individual computer screen could be shown on the IWB screen, allowing you to use this to make a teaching point or to stimulate discussion.

Using an IWB makes it much easier to incorporate ICT into lessons and to demonstrate new ICT skills. There are many occasions when students need to work at their own computers, but equally, there are other occasions when it makes better sense for all the students to be focused on the same computer screen. There is a risk that using ICT will divert students' attention from the subject issues to concerns with ICT skills. Rather than using ICT to enable them to understand a concept better, they worry about which key to press, how to rescue things when suddenly they have something different on their screen from everyone else, which font to use, and so on.

When students work in pairs at individual computers, the teacher can easily find herself rushing round the room from one pair of students to another, unable to spend more than a few seconds with any of them if uproar is not to break out. In an atmosphere like this, there is no opportunity for monitoring, scrutinising or evaluating what the students are doing. Work done may contain factual inaccuracies, or be of questionable relevance to the topic under consideration, with more attention paid to the look of the work than to its content. Discussion between pairs of students at a computer is often about technical issues or arguments, about whose turn it is to control the mouse, rather than the subject matter. Printing out a piece of work can become an end in itself rather than an opportunity for evaluation and reflection.

In contrast, using the IWB to demonstrate what has to be done, or as a focus for discussion of important issues, allows you to direct the students' learning. The ICT then becomes a tool rather than an end in itself. Printing out work or displaying it on the IWB allows students to reconsider and redraft what they have written. Instead of the lesson being a nightmare for the teacher with little real learning occurring, it becomes a genuine opportunity for the students.

The IWB makes it much easier to demonstrate how to use software, but it would be a pity to limit use of the IWB to this, since there is so much more that can be done with it. Data-logging equipment can be used with an IWB in science lessons, or practical skills captured on video camera and displayed on the large IWB screen so that all students can see exactly what you are doing. Indeed, once a demonstration is on video you can show crucial aspects more than once, giving a detailed commentary at the same time, or replay it while students repeat an activity for themselves.

Simulations can help students to understand new concepts. Music software can make them into composers. Word processing software, spreadsheets, dynamic geometry and graphing packages provide opportunities in English and maths. On the internet, students can be taught how to search for suitable websites, or be shown different websites which they can then evaluate. Video and audio clips can be added to presentations, and digital cameras used to add pictures to a resource, or pictures and text scanned in from other sources. The possibilities are almost without limit.

Ownership

Material can be personalised, so that a class has ownership of it in a way that is not normally possible with printed books and worksheets. A particular example of this is given in Chapter 7, where MFL presentations created by students including sound files of them speaking in the target language are described. Files can be saved and printed out to form a portfolio of the students' work. Another example of personalisation could be the construction of a printed book or e-book to record a visit or activity. Students could take photos or video clips to illustrate text and/or a spoken narration.

Teachers can also gain more ownership of their lesson resources. Several teachers told me that they are 'constantly updating and improving' what they do, using tips from other people or finding new techniques. One teacher said it helped her 'to get re-inspired', to see what others are doing and to think about how she could use their ideas in her own teaching.

Creating records and supporting home–school links

The IWB can be used to create and save records or a portfolio of work for each student in the class. Each child's record might contain examples of their work, together with contributions they had made to class discussion, providing an exact, permanent record which can be compared over time and used to facilitate report-writing and discussions at parents' evenings. There is no need to keep lots of books or pieces of paper, just a file on the school network.

Keeping parents up to date with how much their child's work has improved, or not, is easy with the IWB. The student's work can be saved and printed out to be sent home as part of a record of achievement. If the class has been working together on a project that is not portable, then parents may not get a chance to see what their child is doing until there is an open evening or parents' evening. This may be months away, and by then the work may be damaged, broken up or simply no longer be of interest. With an IWB, students can take home a printout of the work they have been doing to carry on with at home, or to show their parents. This facilitates parental involvement in project work, or in appreciating how much a child has improved in some particular aspect.

CHAPTER 3

Pedagogy

Research shows that effective use of ICT requires teachers to think through the pedagogical issues its use raises, and this applies equally to the IWB. The main task for teachers is not to familiarise themselves with the software or the equipment, but to understand how these can contribute to the lesson objectives. Students still need their learning to be monitored and structured, and there still needs to be a clear focus on the subject content. Using ICT or an IWB should offer clear pedagogical gains for the students.

Features of effective teaching include:

- making sure students are aware of the relevance of a lesson to what has gone before, or what is to come;

- checking that the students have any prior knowledge required at the beginning of the lesson;

- well-structured and well-paced lessons;

- high-quality content;

- using questions to find out how well the students understand what is going on and encouraging students to ask questions of their own;

- differentiation to ensure that there are tasks accessible to and appropriate for all students;

- authentic learning tasks which are relevant and interesting to the students;

- clear expectations of all students;

- incorporating students' ideas throughout the planning stage of an activity as well as during it, to maximise students' ownership of what they do;

◉ allowing students to take some responsibility for their own learning by encouraging independent thinking and collaborative work; and

◉ maintaining the students' interest and suiting the needs of different types of learners through the use of a variety of teaching styles and resources.

I have seen several excellent lessons in which the IWB was used as a focus for whole-class teaching and discussion, and then to provide differentiated activities for small groups of students. The IWB supported each phase of the lesson, providing variety and pace. The students clearly enjoyed their lessons; it was equally clear that they were learning and that they were able to articulate what they were learning.

Consider these two lessons. One was a maths lesson, where the teacher was using a flipchart/notebook she had prepared in advance using her IWB software. She had all the pages she was likely to need, plus some spare questions ready for use as required. Each page had several questions for the students to do from which they could choose those appropriate to their understanding of the topic, rather than plodding through an exercise, regardless of its suitability to each individual. Once the teacher thought the students had spent enough time on one particular type of question, she moved them on to a different type, so they were not repeating the same techniques endlessly.

The teacher demonstrated a mathematical proof, with an exact diagram that helped students follow what she was saying. The demonstration was highly visual, well-paced, and gave opportunities for her to ask high-level questions of the students. The students' answers showed they were following the lesson, as did the questions they asked, which were relevant and useful.

The students remained on task throughout the period where they were working independently, with no-one finished because there was nothing left for them to do, or struggling because they did not know how to proceed. The teacher had time to talk to students individually and to follow up their questions with them.

The second lesson was a history lesson where the teacher did not have an IWB available. He had worksheets for the students to use, but he needed to put ideas and instructions on the board as he and the class discussed the tasks to be done. Some students finished the first activity and then just sat talking to their neighbours while they waited. Others lost interest, unsure what to do or unable to read the material provided quickly enough. These students also chatted to their neighbours. Pace was lost again when the teacher drew a picture on the board to motivate the next part of the lesson.

If an IWB had been available all the instructions and drawings could have been immediately ready for the class. Scribbled writing and sketchy drawings would not have been an issue. He could have modelled the activity first, so that those who found it difficult had a clearer idea of what was expected of them. There could also have been one or two extension questions ready to challenge those who finished quickly.

The final activity in the lesson was a series of votes for which individual whiteboards were used. Handing these out and making sure everyone had a suitable felt-tip pen led to loss of pace again, and counting votes was noisy and time-consuming. A voting system, provided by many IWBs, makes this kind of activity much more manageable.

Talking about the lesson afterwards the teacher said he would have loved to have had an IWB available, so that he could have presented materials quickly to the class, leaving him time to work with those who needed more support or more challenging ideas to think about. The class ran out of time before the final activity was completely finished. With an IWB, they could have continued at the start of the next lesson, after a quick reminder about what they were doing. Without an IWB, it is unlikely that they finished the activity at all.

Overall, the maths lesson felt as if the teacher was in control throughout, and that an appropriate pace and focus were maintained. The teacher had time to cover all the aspects of the topic she wanted to, and then there was also time for the students to work on well-chosen follow-up problems that had been clearly modelled for them. During the whole-class part of the lesson, she asked questions which required the students to engage with the material, and to think through the new concepts to which they were being introduced. The students remained focused and on-task.

During the history lesson, the teacher was visibly more rushed, and yet students were frequently off-task, either because they had finished the task or because they did not know how to proceed with it. Pace and focus were lost several times during the lesson, with the teacher then needing to get the students back on task.

Lessons in which an IWB is used generally enable teachers to spend more time engaged with the students, with less time wasted when students are not listening properly or are off-task. Consequently, the relationship between the teacher and students is better. At the end of the lesson, the teacher is less stressed, finding it easier to maintain control, and the students have had a good learning experience.

The IWB as a pedagogical tool

An IWB helps teachers to use a wide variety of different teaching styles, benefiting all types of learners. Our brains access information through visual, auditory and kinaesthetic sensory inputs and these are all available with an IWB. Visual learners can enjoy the colours, graphics, pictures, graphs, mind maps and so on;

kinaesthetic learners will appreciate videos and animations and can touch and move things on the board; audio and video files can be used to supplement classroom discussion to stimulate auditory learners.

Students particularly like the large images and the visual emphasis that the IWB encourages, and many of the students I talked to commented on this. Certainly, the big screen helps students to focus, to maintain their attention and to see text clearly, and the effect of this on their learning should not be underestimated. However, if this is to be made effective, you need to be sure that everything is easily visible from the back of the classroom. This is very straightforward; it merely requires briefly viewing material from the back of the room. It will not take long for you to know the minimum size of font and images that show up clearly. If anything is too small, or if colours do not show up against each other, it is easy to make the necessary changes.

IWB use can help teachers to present their lessons in a structured way, with objectives made clear and links to preceding material emphasised. Hyperlinks can be made to different activities, allowing differentiation and quick access to a variety of resources. Pace can be maintained since everything that is needed in a lesson can be made available at the click of an electronic pen or the tap of a finger. High-quality content and authentic tasks can be resourced in many different ways.

A lesson might start with a review of relevant material covered earlier, using summaries from previous lessons. An outline of what is to be done this lesson, with learning objectives clearly stated, could then follow. Open questions might come next to encourage discussion, and allow for questions and answers from the class. The board can be used to free students from the need to take notes or copy things. Notes can be taken at the board by a 'scribe' (not necessarily the teacher) during discussion and can then be saved and printed out if students need their own copy. If students have discussed with each other and the teacher how they are to set about a task, pace and focus may be better maintained by the students getting on with the task, rather than stopping to make notes on what is to be done.

Once you are ready for the students to move into small groups or individual activity, instructions can be ready on the IWB so that everyone knows what they are to do. Towards the end of the lesson, individual students or groups of students could present their work on the IWB for the class to discuss what has been found out or achieved during the lesson, and to summarise. This would then form the start of the next lesson, with the opportunity to go back over any aspect that students had not properly grasped in the previous lesson.

None of this looks very startling or innovative, although it is clearly useful to be able to review previous material or to look ahead to what is coming. However, the actual content on the IWB at any point could be very different from anything seen on a traditional whiteboard. The files used might contain video, photos, images, text or sound. If an unexpected question highlights the need to diverge from the initial teaching plan, the wealth of resources available on the IWB makes it much easier to react to that question immediately, instead of saying 'Good question! I'll come back to that'.

Using an IWB means that work in progress can be kept so that it is ready as a starting point the next time the class works on that particular topic. This facilitates projects that last longer than one lesson, since everything that is on the IWB can be saved, and printed out if required. There is no danger of it getting lost or damaged, and everyone can have access to everything that has been done. Each student can take home the entire project if they want to, for further work or to share with parents.

Redefining the position of the teacher in relation to the learning process of the student

This comment was made by a maths teacher who had been using an IWB for two and a half years. He continued:

> It enables the teacher to learn with the student when the technology delivers the learning . . . You can help them much better if you don't spend all your time writing on the board, and if there's an awareness of the technology delivering the answer, and the student and the teacher sharing in the discovery of the answer. [This can be] very motivating for a low achieving group. Technology lets the student test a working hypothesis.

'Technology redefines the position of the teacher in relation to the learning process of the student.'

He felt that the IWB could relocate the teacher in the relationship between a student and new knowledge. He emphasised that he did not mean by this that the technology took over, and he was clear that he remained in control of the learning process. Nevertheless, he felt that the technology could become the expert, allowing him to share with his students the excitement of making new discoveries.

He was not alone in making this particular point. Many teachers like the fact that they do not always have to take the role of the expert or be the person who leads everything. When students present their work at the board, or when it confirms that their answers are correct, it gives them the confidence to go on and learn more. They can take an active part in the teaching process, demonstrating concepts or ideas to their peers.

This particular teacher linked the change in her role brought about by the IWB with a change in the way the students were learning. She had noticed an increase in the proportion of students prepared to come out and have a go at the board, because they could undo things quickly, helping them to accept errors. She felt

'It's the getting involved . . . It's the sharing aspect, and getting up and working on the board in a social environment. That's what makes the difference. While they are at the board, they can . . . move things around . . . and the other kids [are] watching and taking part. The class will be watching, chipping in, asking questions, making a consensus of what we believe to be right. My job is to use questions to steer them in that right direction. They take part in the whole thing. A Year 11 kid said: "I always understood where I'd been, and where I was going in your lessons". The board allows you to do that.'

this had reduced social issues for the less confident students. She ended by saying:

'We've had kids come up and make some quite profound reasoning who never came up to the board before.'

The IWB also enables teachers to model good learning styles to their students. As teachers we need to set a good example: we need to be prepared to try something new, to experiment, to laugh if we make mistakes. Learning new things requires you to put in time and effort, and seeing adults do this is good for students. It encourages them to give things a go. Teachers are no more infallible than students and we should not be afraid to admit it.

'What's the whole premise of education? We're saying to them, you can do this. But if we're not prepared to have a go with new technology, how can we expect kids to have a go at something far more unfamiliar!'

Teaching style

The IWB is often used for whole-class teaching or for working with groups of students around the board. Whole-class teaching has been emphasised by the three-part lesson structure, particularly at the beginning and end of the lesson, and an IWB is ideal for this aspect of teaching. However, there is a risk that the

IWB will encourage teachers to spend too long at the front, transmitting information or instructing the students, and not enough time letting them work individually or in small groups. Critics of IWB technology have claimed that it encourages direct instruction at the expense of students being actively involved in their own learning.

There is no reason why IWB use should contribute to the greater use of direct instruction than was previously the case, however. If the IWB is used for long sessions of direct instruction, then teaching style should be reconsidered, as the novelty value of a board used in this way will soon wear off. However, many teachers find there are more opportunities to involve the students with an IWB, so that there is more participation than previously, and the students are now keener to contribute: 'They will run the show if you let them'.

It is in any case a fallacy that the IWB can only be used for whole-class work. For instance, the IWB can be used with small groups, by making different programs available simultaneously on the board, so that students can use them as they want for individual work. Another possibility is to get small groups working around an IWB tablet or a computer from which they can send material to the server, and hence display it on the IWB.

An emphasis on whole-class teaching is not a bad thing – it is direct instruction at the expense of students being active in their own learning which needs to be avoided. Teachers need to take charge of discussion with and between students if they are to remain focused and if they are to listen to each other properly. Enabling and monitoring whole-class discussion is, after all, an integral aspect of teaching, and the IWB has much to offer in facilitating such discussion.

The IWB takes the place of the ordinary whiteboard or overhead projector at the front of the class for occasions when you want all the students focused on the same thing. The whole class can then concentrate together on the same thing, whereas if students are looking at pieces of paper or books in front of them, they may be looking at something quite different. If students do not have to keep switching their attention from you to a book and back again, there is less likelihood that they will be distracted by something else going on in the room or outside, helping them to concentrate for longer.

Whether the IWB is used with a whole class or with a small group, it can and should be used by the students to encourage them to contribute to the lesson. As a Year 7 student put it:

> 'They're good because you can do things with them, as normally you would just have a teacher writing on the board, but with an IWB you all get a go.'

For example, using an IWB can facilitate brainstorming an activity. When everyone has had their say, the suggestions can be tidied up, saved for another day and/or printed out for everyone to work on. You could convert the ideas to a mind map or present them to the class as a plan of action for a subsequent lesson.

To facilitate such discussion it may be preferable to use a wireless keyboard, wireless mouse or an IWB tablet or slate so that students can put things on the board without leaving their seats, thus avoiding streams of students coming out in turn to put something on the board, leading to a slow pace and the opportunity for distraction. Alternatively, students can take turns to be the scribe, working directly at the board.

Increased student participation has to be a good thing however it is achieved.

'I always had a lot of participation with pupils coming up to demonstrate how to do things. The IWB has increased that – boys like to use the IWB, and they pay more attention in class now, because they want to see how it works. They watch carefully when you are teaching so they can use tools in their own presentations. It's helped introduce a bit more laughter too. They expect it to be hard, and it isn't. They laugh at their handwriting, and so on, but it's good laughter – it lightens up the mood a bit. Games are really good: kids love using them. They can work in teams without supervision once they know the game.'

The physical interaction of going up to the board to touch and move things about is an important way for students to manipulate objects and to demonstrate their ideas. Similarly, using highlighting, adding words or moving them about help students to engage with text. Boys are often less reluctant to come up to the IWB than they are with an ordinary whiteboard because it is a computer and they enjoy the involvement with the technology.

Motivating learning

'. . . we discuss questions a lot more – we get more time to talk. The "why is this happening?" type of question has become "what if" because there are so many examples available. They participate better, even the worst pupils. They don't mind asking a question, because the answer is quick, immediate. It doesn't matter if you ask – it's only 30 seconds, not a long explanation with everyone else thinking "why doesn't he or she understand that?".'

Using an IWB increases the pace and depth of lessons and gives more time for discussion and questioning. The emphasis moves from writing the question down and copying it, to brainstorming ideas. This helps students to focus on understanding the lesson content and sharing ideas, rather than concentrating on getting things written down. In some classes, the increased depth means that fewer problems are tackled as they become vehicles for discussing concepts, rather than just practising techniques, but that students gain more from this approach.

Students' attention is not lost by having to clean the board and start over again, losing what has gone before. Indeed, there may be far less need to write on the board at all. Because all the resources that are needed for a lesson can be prepared ahead of time, and presented on the IWB, time is saved in having students hand out books or worksheets and find the right page, or in having to write up material or draw diagrams. Everything is ready on demand. This means that you can explain quickly and efficiently what you want the class to do, so that there is more time for students to work independently or in small groups, and for you to discuss concepts with them, rather than give instructions.

These comments from Year 7 students demonstrate how motivating they find its use:

'I enjoy using the IWB . . . Without it lessons wouldn't be as [much] fun because you can use programs that make the lessons interesting and easier to understand.'

'It is good because you can see things instead of having to imagine them; you can find out more because you are linked to a computer and have internet access.'

Teachers also think IWB use is motivating:

'They work more quickly and are more aware. They want to go up levels, to see what the highest-level work looks like. They see more and find out more, they don't want to miss out.'

'At KS3 and 4, I have some classes where most of the lessons are in my own classroom, but with one or two a fortnight elsewhere. There's a feeling of something missing for the students – a focus of excitement, a Pandora's box – a lot of things could come out of it. It's a box of delights. It comes back to student motivation. We forget what motivates children – a sense of excitement – a feeling of new worlds opening up. Properly used, an IWB can be used to keep that sense of excitement alive.'

Will the novelty wear off? The classes I observed had all been exposed to IWB use for some time, and there was no sign that this was the case. Provided that the teacher was using appropriate resources which the students found stimulating, their interest was maintained. After all, the IWB is not just a single resource; it is a whole host of resources, so there is no reason why time should affect their value. The usefulness of the IWB depends entirely on the quality of the resources used, and that is a pedagogical issue rather than a technological one.

Inclusion

How's this for a way to recapture the interest of students who have become distracted? Open up a digital photo of the class (one taken earlier and saved in your files), open the Spotlight tool and move it around so that it shows the students who are not paying attention. It won't be long before they are!

An IWB is a marvellous tool for inclusion. It can engage students, regardless of ability, learning needs or language difficulties, through the seamless use of different resources, and give a focus for everyone in the class. The IWB can also be used to leave a presentation playing, providing a reminder for others on the content of a lesson, while you work with individual students or small groups. All learners can be supported through the provision of visual or aural stimuli, and the IWB can further be used to give a calm, studious feel to a room by playing background music while students work. IWB use can also help teachers to provide greater support for students who have special needs or who have become demotivated.

With the IWB as a focus, everyone in the class can contribute to discussion and have their contribution celebrated. Because students' work can be displayed in multimedia form to everyone, those who find it a struggle to create texts can present their ideas to the whole class using graphics, photos, sound or video. Students can learn from each other by listening to others talk about what they have done, how they did it and why – a benefit for all, regardless of ability.

Using an IWB allows you to provide resources that are not otherwise available. On the BBC website alone there are animations of Stevenson's *Rocket*, panoramas of historic rooms and virtual reality reconstructions of places such as London Bridge in the sixteenth century that students can 'walk' through. Other websites provide beating hearts, live broadcasts from webcams of African waterholes or images of distant planets. The British Pathé Archive has many hours of video that schools can use. More suggestions are given in Appendix 1.

Many IWBs also have interactive voting tools available. Students have a handheld device which they use to choose answers from a selection shown on the IWB. These can be used for formative assessment, so that you know how individual students perform on key questions, as well as how the whole class is progressing. Such systems can also be used to save students being embarrassed or refusing to reply at all if they are reluctant to answer publicly, or if questions are of a sensitive nature.

All of us have different ways of learning, broadly categorised as visual – what we see; auditory – what we hear; and kinaesthetic – what we do. Of course, we do not learn in just one way: all of us learn in all these ways and will switch between styles depending upon the task. The challenge is to teach to the different learning styles so that the needs of all the learners present are met. The use of visual and auditory stimuli helps in this, as does the opportunity to use the mouse pen or the finger to move objects around the board. Students can pick up text and move it around to change the sense of a sentence, or to put it in its proper order. They can draw diagrams, and then move lines about to see what difference it makes. Objects can be dragged across the screen to sort them or match them with other objects. Creating mind maps (using specialist software or tools available in IWB software) can help students to scaffold and structure their thinking, either as a means of supporting memory or of ordering thoughts prior to writing or making presentations.

The visual impact of the whiteboard is obvious: it gives an immediate, brightly lit, difficult-to-ignore focus at the front of the room, allowing even the densest of texts to be made more accessible. The teacher can lead a discussion of what is on screen, reading it aloud, perhaps, for those with reading difficulties, using IWB tools to support this process. The highlighter (from the IWB tools or in Word) can be used to pick out key features – a rhyming scheme for instance – making it multicoloured and so more obvious. The pen tool can be used to underline and link words or the spotlight tool used to pick out individual words for discussion. Any page that has been annotated can then be printed out for further use.

Students for whom English is not their first language, or who have emotional and behavioural difficulties, may find using digital video helpful. Using video to record themselves or to film role-plays or stories they have written can help students to talk about themselves and their experiences, which impacts on language use and development. It can also help students to express their feelings about difficult or emotional events. Creativity and collaboration are emphasised in projects like this, which can help students to establish better relationships with their peers and teachers. Video clips can be presented via the IWB to the rest of the class or used as part of ongoing work using other media.

For students who are visually impaired the sheer size of the content can make it easier to see, as can the range of colours and different pen widths available. Students with some form of dyslexia might be helped by using non-standard colours, such as cream text on a dark blue background. Colours can be specifically chosen to support such students. Similarly, students with hearing impairments can see transcripts of speeches or videos displayed on the board while they listen; and all learners will benefit from being able to hear soundtracks properly through a good speaker system. Adding appropriate images and sound effects to a presentation will give students another hook on which to hang their learning, a reference point for their memories.

The addition of other tools to the IWB, such as infra-red keyboards or graphics tablets, and access devices such as a gyroscopic mouse, makes it even more powerful. All these mean that students can operate the board from their own seats. Pace is not lost while someone gets up and walks to the front, and those with mobility problems can make a full contribution to the lesson. Students who find it difficult to work with a pen may find types of IWBs/tablets that allow use of the fingers helpful. Students could produce their own pictures to illustrate their work, using their fingers to draw on the board or by importing clipart. Many boards also have handwriting recognition, which could aid some students. They can write directly on the board with their fingers and the handwriting recognition tool can then convert this to text.

As a means of including all students in learning, the interactive whiteboard is a powerful addition to the teacher's toolbox. It can help to engage students, to motivate them and to develop their understanding through opening up the topic being studied, and it will enhance collaboration and therefore learning between students. The capacity to provide media-rich materials can support all students regardless of how they prefer to learn or of their various learning difficulties.

Student achievement

Increasing student motivation and engagement in learning should lead to increased achievement by all students. If the students are paying more attention to the subject matter, more of it will be absorbed. If they experience visual or auditory stimuli, or can work at the board, they are more likely to remember lessons. In several schools, over the period that they have used IWBs, their Key Stage 3 results have improved noticeably. Indeed, IWB use has allowed some teachers to accelerate classes, so that they can take GCSEs a year early or spend more time on enrichment activities.

In one particular school I visited, teachers looked at the results for a particular topic for their Year 8 groups and found that those who used IWBs had obviously enjoyed the topic more and got more out of it. Their routine work was similar to the other students, but the students in classes using IWBs coped better with higher-order questions. If these students were given enough time 'they could work through it better, had more reasoning – not enough to show a significantly better result over all, but on individual questions, a much better reasoning'. At this school, their Key Stage 3 SATs results had been 'absolutely outstanding' that year, and they were convinced that this must have something to do with the use of the IWB.

Good and bad practice with the IWB

Describing good practice, this teacher emphasised:

> 'The really important thing to remember is that the point is interacting. Kids have to interact – get up there, touch things, move things, be enthusiastic and try things. Things that are good practice with an IWB are those things that make you a good teacher. You have to look for new things, re-evaluate.'

Good practice means using the technology to do things that are worth doing. An IWB means you can make lesson content lively, with movement, sound and colour used creatively. The technology should bring the topic alive for the students, not hide it in technological wizardry. It is important that the technology is not used just because it is there, but because it has something to offer. Other than that, the criteria for good practice with an IWB are generally the same as for any other teaching.

One area where the IWB can make a specific contribution is in enabling teachers to help students to see the part in the context of the whole by going back to previous pages, by showing a multi-page view or by using a mind map to show how the parts make up the whole. Students need to be reminded of the steps they went through in order to learn something, as well as the sum total of what they have learned.

A different aspect of good practice concerns filing lesson resources. Building up a bank of two-week topics, rather than a proliferation of little things, helps you to keep track of what you have and how it fits into the scheme of work in your department. It can be difficult to manage a rapidly increasing archive of resources and students' work, and this needs careful consideration. It is important to have a filing system that works for the whole department so that everyone knows what is in a resource, where it is and how to find it quickly.

Other features of good practice at the IWB include not using too much text, using lots of images, highlighting things so that they have real impact and using colour for emphasis. Making sure font sizes and colours stand out, so that the students can see everything clearly from the back of the classroom, is obviously important too.

Regarding bad practice, if the students do not understand the lesson, and it does not open up the subject matter to them, then it is a wasted opportunity. More specific instances of bad practice include using the IWB as 'a textbook on the wall', where students have little or no opportunity to engage with the subject matter. Too much text or handwriting is a waste of the IWB's facilities and is likely to bore the students. Text can be prepared in advance so that it is typed, visible and broken up into manageable chunks for further analysis or discussion using the IWB tools. Visual distractions, like images that are not aligned when they should be, squares that are not square and lines that are not straight, should also be avoided.

Many teachers told me of instances of people using an IWB as an ordinary whiteboard, not bothering to find out what it could do. They viewed such examples as poor practice, showing a lack of commitment by the teachers involved.

'It's bad to stagnate, to use the board intermittently, not taking the time to learn things, using it as just another board.'

PART 2

Creating Lesson Resources

This part of the book contains technical details of how to use various forms of software, including Microsoft Word, PowerPoint, Excel and Paint, and the IWB software for the SMARTBoard, Promethean's ACTIVstudio2 and the Hitachi StarBoard. It also shows how such software can be used to create interesting lesson content.

Many of the technical instructions on how to perform operations are shown in the margins rather than in the main text. There are four possible ways to carry out operations: by clicking on icons on toolbars, by using right-mouse clicks (either on the board or on the computer), by accessing drop-down menus and by keyboard shortcuts, although all these alternatives may not exist for a specific operation. When an IWB is used with a class, the icons and mouse clicks are probably the quickest way to do things; in preparation, keyboard shortcuts, where these exist, are probably quickest. In the margins, icons and mouse clicks are given first and then menu instructions, shown in normal text, and finally keyboard shortcuts are shown in italic text.

Right-mouse click
Menu instructions
Keyboard shortcuts

Specific techniques are described in the context of teaching materials, all of which are available on the accompanying CD. Many of these techniques are useful in several curriculum areas, so they are not presented by subject content but by teaching technique or strategy. Some of the resources provide exemplars rather than materials to be used with a class. The resources on the CD can be used as they are, if appropriate, or edited so that their content reflects directly the objectives and content of a specific lesson. The Word document *Notes_on_resources.doc* on the CD gives details of the content of the files.

Various attempts have been made to identify stages in the development of teachers' use of an IWB. One such schema identifies familiarisation, utilisation, integration, reorientation and evolution. Teachers go through familiarisation when they first begin to find out what the IWB can do. Utilisation occurs when they start to use the board in the classroom by replacing things they would previously have done without it. This may seem unnecessary use – surely ICT should only be used if there is some clear advantage to be gained from that use? Apart from helping to reach higher stages, however, this stage may not be without its own benefits. The pace of lessons may increase through the ready availability of other resources; higher-order questions may be provoked by such resources; annotated documents can be saved for future use.

A real difference occurs on reaching the stage of integration. At this stage, teachers regard the board as a necessary part of their teaching resources, and would not consider being deprived of it.

A teacher at this stage can see that the IWB offers many possibilities, and that lesson planning and preparation is stimulated and inspired by these. He or she will incorporate IWB use into lesson planning across the whole range of topics taught.

'Without the IWB I'd still do my job, but it makes it easier. The reflective aspect of the lesson would be harder but possible. But I'd be unhappy.'

Those who have reached the stage of reorientation are prepared to show others how to use it, demonstrating how to use it in their lessons. One teacher told me that she is now training other people. She had had an opportunity to do a presentation on using ICT at a conference and was getting her name known. She was excited by the professional development opportunities that IWB use was making possible.

Finally, those who reach the stage of evolution are the teachers who evolve new ways of presenting material across the curriculum. Such a teacher will integrate ideas and various electronic resources to meet the needs of all the students in her class, always looking out for new ideas and new ways of exploiting the technology available to her so that she improves students' learning experiences. In the lessons I observed, I saw evidence of this: the lessons were fast-paced and exciting, full of good questions and answers from the students.

This part of the book is aimed at beginners and those in the early stages of IWB use, however, rather than those who are already expert. In Chapter 4, detailed instructions are given for carrying out common operations, such as saving and printing, moving from one application to another, preparing templates and worksheets and using the IWB annotation tools. In Chapter 5, Word, PowerPoint, Excel and Paint are considered in more detail, and Chapter 6 covers IWB software. Chapter 7 describes various teaching strategies which can be used with an IWB, and lesson resources which exemplify them. Finally, Chapter 8 gives examples of other software packages which are useful with an IWB.

CHAPTER 4

Getting acquainted with the interactive whiteboard

Getting going

To get started, connect the IWB to the computer and then turn on the computer – most boards need to be connected to the computer first so that the computer registers the presence of the IWB during its start-up procedure. When the computer is ready, the IWB will need to be oriented or calibrated. This is normally done by following on-screen instructions to tap crosses or dots with the IWB pen or finger. Once this is done, the point of the on-screen cursor will correspond to the tip of the pen or finger. If you find that your pen/finger tip no longer corresponds to the point of the on-screen cursor during operation, quickly recalibrating the board will solve the problem.

Once the board is set up, try opening an application or website and instead of operating the computer from the keyboard, do it at the board using the special pen or your finger. Once you feel ready to use the board in class, a good place to start is with an internet site or an application already familiar to you and your class. This enables the novice IWB user to concentrate on operating the board with a well-known activity. Interactive games gain from being displayed to the whole class on the IWB, and these might provide a good first step. It helps if you open the website or the program prior to the start of the lesson, so that a tap or click will bring it up, ready for use. Finding websites can be time-consuming, so bookmarking websites you like, saving them in 'Favourites', or having them available off-line where they can be quickly accessed, is also useful.

Displaying resources is helped if the toolbars are not visible when they are not needed. If a website is viewed through Internet Explorer, tapping F11 on the keyboard will remove the toolbars at the top of the page, making the content much clearer. Tapping it again will bring the toolbars back. Many other documents, including Word and Excel, can be viewed Full Screen, which is normally to be found through the View

> **Full screen view**
> **IE:**
> F11
> **Word, Excel:**
> View>
> Full Screen

menu on the top toolbar. Using Full Screen will remove all the toolbars, leaving just a small floating toolbar which can be moved to a convenient place on the screen (see Figure 7.9, p.101). Clicking or tapping on this or pressing the 'Esc' key will restore the normal view.

Common operations

Generally speaking, Microsoft Office applications (such as Word, PowerPoint and Excel), MS Paint and SMARTBoard notebooks all function in much the same way. The SMARTBoard has more or less the same menu options as those described for MS applications, the icons are very similar and the standard keyboard shortcuts can be used. Promethean ACTIVstudio2 (AS2) and Hitachi StarBoards are rather different. In the following sections, you can assume that all of the above applications/software act in the way described, unless a different method of performing an operation is given for a particular type of software. If you are unsure what a particular icon does, hover the mouse above it for a few seconds. The name of the icon should show, and often this will be sufficient to explain what it does.

Saving and printing

Save

File>Save
File>Save As (to save under another name/location)
Control (Ctrl) S
Print

File>Print
Ctrl P

Flipchart>
Save to
Flipchart>Print

View>PageList

Almost all software applications use the same methods for common operations like saving and printing. There are usually three ways to carry out such operations. On the second bar from the top (the top bar gives the name of the file), there are drop-down menus labelled File, Edit, View and so on, and saving and printing are normally to be found in the File menu. Short-cut icons for the most common operations can be found on the third bar down from the top of the screen, and short-cut keyboard strokes can also be used. The SMARTBoard has a Save icon very similar to the one shown in the margin, but no Print icon.

As with much of what follows, AS2 and StarBoard software are rather different – neither have top toolbars with menus or icons, but use icons on floating toolbars, some of which link to menus or dialogue boxes. You can drag icons from the menus or toolboxes to the floating toolbar to make common operations quicker. To save or print a flipchart in AS2, click on the Promethean man symbol at the top left of the floating toolbar. This gives the main menu for AS2, which can be used to access Save and Print options. To save or print a StarBoard flipchart, click on the Page List icon on the floating toolbar to access a dialogue box. Make sure Capture Images is selected, then click on Save or Print. When saving, you have the option of choosing either Save or Export to a File. If you choose Save, you will save your flipchart to the Favourites folder in the StarBoard software, whereas choosing Export to a File allows you to select your own folder. Opening StarBoard flipcharts is easier from the Favourites folder, so you may want to keep all your files there for ease of navigation during lessons.

Moving from one application to another

One of the advantages of using an IWB is that you can move very quickly between computer applications. This means you can access different resources as often as you want during a lesson. Try opening two or three different documents from your Windows desktop. There should be a taskbar at the bottom of the screen with the Start button on the left, then tabs for all the open applications other than the StarBoard. The tab for the application that is currently active will have a darker background colour than the rest. To move to a different application (except AS2 and the StarBoard), just click on its tab.

To access an AS2 flipchart, use the Flipchart icon on the floating toolbar; this icon can be used to toggle back and forth between a flipchart and any other application or website. To access a StarBoard flipchart, click the Page List icon on the floating toolbar, select Capture Images in the dialogue box and then double click on the required page. To go back to another application, click on the PC icon on the floating toolbar.

Flipchart icon

View>PageList

Mode>PC screen

Copy/cut and paste

Copying or cutting then pasting text or pictures from one page to another or from one application to another is a very common operation. Cutting removes an object from its current position while copying leaves it in place. Start by selecting the object or text to be cut or copied, then follow the instructions in the margin to remove or copy the selected material to the Windows 'clipboard'. Once something is on the clipboard, it is accessible from any application in Windows. To paste an object from the clipboard into another document, or into the same document in a different place, go to the point where you want the cut or copied material to go, then use the paste icon (or alternative). The text or picture should appear in its new position. The SMARTBoard has a Paste icon very similar to the one shown, but no Cut or Copy icons – you will need to access these via the drop-down menus. Right-clicking also gives Paste but not Cut or Copy; however, the keyboard shortcuts all work on the SMARTBoard.

As usual, the only applications where this procedure is somewhat different are AS2 and the StarBoard, although both allow text to be copied and pasted in text boxes using the Ctrl C and Ctrl V keyboard shortcuts. To cut or copy an object in AS2, select it and then right-click on it (there is a button on the pen which gives a right-click, or use the right-hand mouse button). A short toolbar with an 'M' in the top left corner will appear. Click on the 'M' to produce another menu from which options to Edit, which includes

Cut

Right-click>Cut
Edit>Cut
Ctrl X
Copy

Right-click>Copy
Edit>Copy
Ctrl C
Paste

Right-click>Paste
Edit>Paste
Ctrl V

Cut
M>Edit>Cut
Copy
M>Edit>Copy
Paste
M>Paste

35

Edit>Cut

Edit>Copy

Edit>Paste

Cut and Copy, can be selected. To paste an object onto a flipchart page in AS2, cut or copy it to the clipboard, then return to the flipchart, right-click on the page to give the menu and then click on the 'M'. Choosing Paste will give options to choose between objects on the clipboard for pasting. To cut or copy objects on the StarBoard, select them, then use the icons on the floating toolbar or the StarBoard Edit menu. To paste an object to a flipchart, cut or copy it to the clipboard, then return to the flipchart and use the Paste icon on the toolbar or the Edit menu.

Another way to copy an object from a flipchart/notebook to a different location is to use the ScreenCapture tool to take a snapshot of the object. The snapshot can be pasted directly to another page in the flipchart/notebook, or to the clipboard for pasting into a different application. Using the ScreenCapture tool is described in more detail in Chapter 6 for the individual types of IWB software.

Annotation tools

The next step is to use the special annotation tools provided in the IWB software with an internet site or familiar resource. Most boards will provide many different tools, but basic ones to try out first are the:

⊙ Pen

⊙ Highlighter

⊙ Eraser

⊙ Undo and Redo

⊙ Clear or Clear Screen

⊙ Screen Capture

Most IWBs are likely to have many other tools, but these are a good basic set to start with. Any or all of these tools can be used with any piece of software, not just with the IWB's own software. Figure 4.1 shows an IWB screen containing text which has been annotated with the annotation tools.

Here, the StarBoard pen/highlighter tool has been used to annotate a flipchart page, but this could just as easily be any other type of IWB pen and/or highlighter with a different application, such as a Word document, a spreadsheet or PowerPoint presentation, or a website. The pen, highlighter and eraser tools can be given different widths and colours for emphasis and clarity. Deciding whether to let the annotations be removed or whether to save them as part of the Word document for future use (see the specific instructions in Chapter 6 for different IWBs) is entirely up to you.

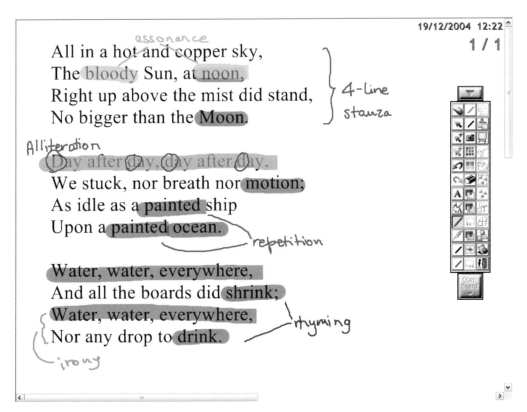

Figure 4.1 Using the IWB annotation tools on a Word document

To start annotating a document on a SMARTBoard, in AS2 or on a StarBoard, make sure the floating toolbar is visible, and that the appropriate tool is selected – for example, the pen or highlighter – then just start annotating. Use the eraser, Clear or Undo icons to remove annotation. The icons to use to stop annotation and return to the live desktop are shown in the margin.

AS2 – Windows icon

StarBoard – PC icon

SMARTboard – Select arrow

The eraser, the Clear screen and the Undo tools have different effects in different software applications, and you will need to experiment to see what they do on your IWB. A basic difference between the eraser tool on the SMARTBoard and the StarBoard compared to the AS2 eraser is that it actually removes annotations, whereas in AS2 the eraser paints a layer over what is underneath. This means that the SMARTBoard and StarBoard erasers, unlike the AS2 eraser, can be used to remove part of an object which will then remain permanently erased. However, dragging the eraser layer aside to reveal hidden text or images is a useful strategy in the classroom, since a complete resource can be prepared with some objects hidden ready to be shown when appropriate. This technique is discussed further in Chapter 7. The Undo and Clear tools remove content in all cases.

Creating templates and worksheets

It is very easy to create illustrations from drawings, photos or clipart with an IWB, providing many ideas for templates and worksheets. Anything that can be produced on an IWB can be saved for future use, or printed out and duplicated for the class. There will be many backgrounds available in the IWB software (see some examples in Figure 4.2), and others can be added to these. Details on how to find these backgrounds in IWB software are given in Chapter 6.

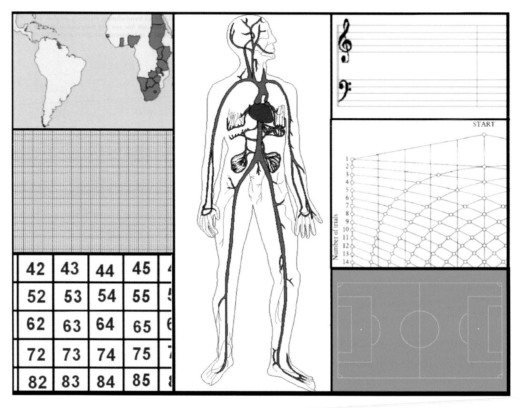

Figure 4.2 Examples of backgrounds available in IWB software

Inserting pictures

If a digital camera is not available, getting one should be a priority for anyone using an IWB. In addition, a wide range of clipart and images is available from the clipart folders in MS Office and the StarBoard, the Gallery on the SMARTBoard and the Resource Library in AS2.

Insert>Picture> From file

Insert>Picture> Clip Art

Inserting photos, picture files and clipart is done in the same way in most applications. Either copy the picture and paste it into the new document, or use the Insert menu on the top toolbar. Clicking on Insert>Pictures gives a range of alternatives. Selecting Clipart opens clipart files and a picture can then be opened in the document, or dragged into it. Selecting Insert>Pictures> From file opens a box which will allow you to navigate to and then open any picture files you may have on your computer. The Insert Picture and Insert Clipart icons are on the toolbar at the bottom of the page in Word, PowerPoint and Excel. Another alternative is to add a picture directly from a scanner or digital camera, and again there is an option for this. Photos and images from a file, camera or scanner can be inserted onto a SMARTBoard page using the Insert menu. Things are slightly different in AS2 and on the StarBoard. The easiest way to incorporate a picture from outside AS2 or the StarBoard into a flipchart is to copy it from the original source or take a snapshot of it with the ScreenCapture tool and then to paste it into the flipchart.

Once a picture has been inserted into a document, it can be resized by dragging the handles on the sides and corners of the picture (little circles usually, which appear when a picture is tapped or clicked with the pen/finger). Using just the handles on the corners will maintain the width:height ratio of the picture. Dragging on either of the side or bottom handles will distort the picture. The SMARTBoard is slightly different in that there is only one handle to drag on, which is to be found at the bottom right of the picture. Dragging this diagonally maintains the width:height ratio, while dragging it horizontally or vertically distorts it.

Creating presentations

IWBs allow the use of two different types of presentation software. All types of IWB can be used for PowerPoint displays, but IWB software also provides its own type of presentation software (the 'whiteboard'). Both these types of software enable you to produce your own resources, containing as many slides or pages as you want. Creating presentations is probably the most time-consuming aspect of using an IWB. Like everything else, however, practice makes perfect, or at least means that interesting lesson resources are much quicker to make. The bonus is that once a resource has been made, it can be permanently saved for future use.

Slides/pages in these presentations can have special backgrounds or designs to create a professional look. Links to websites and other files, including sound and video files, can be added, or pictures and photos inserted. You can also create simple animations in PowerPoint. It takes longer to learn how to create an effective presentation than to use the IWB annotation tools, but a good presentation provides an excellent environment for innovative use of the IWB.

The IWB software will enable you to display large, bright, accurate, attractive pictures, maps and graphs. These can all be resized or moved across the screen; on most boards, shapes can be rotated, and on some they can also be reflected. Scenes can be displayed either as pictures or as video for imaginative work or analysis. Musical instruments or notes could be displayed while a sound file plays so students can hear and see the music and instruments simultaneously.

IWB presentations also provide a way of making other resources accessible to the whole class. Old worksheets and transparencies can be scanned into the computer, then brightened up by changing black and white text to bold, colourful text on a coloured background, with additional pictures added. Internet sites which have text too small to be seen from the back of the classroom, or where there is a lot of irrelevant material, can be transformed into presentations.

When creating a presentation, it is as well to avoid the temptation to make it say everything. It is better to leave gaps – to have open questions, unannotated diagrams, empty maps and so on, so that there is room for you and your class together to fill the spaces. Hyperlinks can allow a lesson to take off in different ways, rather than simply following a linear path. Leaving room for students to participate in a presentation and using links allows you to follow different pathways, depending on where class discussion goes on a given day.

Presentations require visual issues to be carefully considered. IWBs are meant to give excellent visual display, but this will not occur if there is bright sunlight shining on the board. A dark-coloured background may help, with pale colours for text and images. Lack of contrast can also be a reason for visibility problems; deep colours do not show up against other deep colours, and pale colours do not show up against other pale colours. It is a good idea to have a deep colour for the background or the text and a pale colour for the other. Colours which are opposite each other in the colour spectrum, such as blue/orange or purple/yellow, show up well against each other. Green/red is a special case, however, as some students may have green/red colour blindness. Many students with dyslexia find that pale yellow or cream text against a dark blue background (or vice versa) helps them to see things more clearly. Other students with dyslexia may prefer other colour schemes. If there is such a student in your class, you can make sure that colour schemes support this student's visual abilities, rather than the reverse.

Use of additional ICT

Scanner

To make the most of an IWB, a scanner is absolutely essential so that you can make use of printed and hand-produced material. A scanner enables you to scan text or images, including students' work, into the computer for display on the IWB. This can be seen in the resources in Chapter 7, where students' drawings have been scanned for use in a PowerPoint resource, together with sound files they recorded.

Cameras, videos and sound

Like a scanner, a digital camera and/or video recorder will add variety to the resources that you can use with an IWB. Digital cameras can be used to add photos taken of or by the students around the school or on trips out of school. Video files and sound files can be added to most presentation software and can be played directly from the IWB, without the need to find additional hardware. Video clips can be annotated in the same way that text or images can, and the resulting file saved for later use. Digital video clips could be made by the students, or could show them doing a role-play or presenting information. Students can make their own sound files as well as using those available in PowerPoint or in the IWB software, adding a completely new dimension to a lesson. Alternatively, music can be played while students complete individual tasks, helping them to concentrate rather than chat. Using additional ICT in this way will not only add hugely to the interest of resources, but will also give you and your students ownership of their lesson materials.

To create reasonable sound or video files, you need a fast computer with a sound card, software such as Windows Media Player, RealPlayer or QuickTime, and a good microphone. Poor-quality audio is a common problem in sound and video files, and is often due to a poor-quality microphone. Attach the microphone to the pink socket on the PC or laptop.

The Windows Sound Recorder can be used to record sound files, and some types of IWB have their own sound recording software. To use the Windows Sound Recorder, open it up, then press Record (the button with a red spot on it) and start recording. When the recording is complete, save the file and play it through to check that the sound levels are all right. The  person recording may need to put the microphone a little closer to them or a little further away if the sound is too soft or too loud. To access an existing sound file, use File>Open and then press the Play button.

To make a video file, you will need a digital video camera. Follow the instructions with your camera to produce and save a file. Attaching sound and video files to presentations is described in Chapters 5 and 6 in the detailed instructions on using various applications.

CHAPTER 5

Microsoft software

This chapter gives an overview of some useful common functions for readers who are inexperienced with Microsoft software. Further help is usually quite easy to find on the internet or in the user manual if your school has one.

Handy shortcuts

There are several standard Windows keyboard shortcuts that you can use in Microsoft applications to speed up preparation:

- Ctrl Z – undoes your last action
- Ctrl Y – repeats your last action
- Ctrl S – saves the document currently open
- Ctrl P – prints the document currently open
- Ctrl N – opens a new document
- Ctrl O – opens an existing document
- Ctrl C – copies
- Ctrl X – cuts
- Ctrl V – pastes
- Ctrl A – selects everything in a Word file, on a spreadsheet worksheet or on a PowerPoint slide
- Ctrl I – italic font
- Ctrl B – bold font

- Ctrl U – underlines

- Ctrl F – gives a dialogue box which you can use to Find specific text

- Ctrl G – gives a dialogue box which you can use to Go To a specific point in a document

- Ctrl H – gives a dialogue box which you can use to Replace specific text

- Ctrl K – gives a dialogue box which you can use to insert a Hyperlink to another document or elsewhere in the same document

Word

Word, from Microsoft Office, is a form of word-processing software. Its main use is in processing text, but you can also insert pictures and draw in Word. Word can be used in the classroom to demonstrate to students how to draft and edit a piece of work, as in Figure 5.1.

Here a short passage written by a student just starting French is shown with corrections inserted. This technique can be used in any curriculum area where work needs to be drafted and redrafted, and corrections discussed. Text can be shown as the original, original showing mark-up, final or final showing mark-up. These options can be found in a box on the toolbar just above the

Tools>Track
Changes
Ctrl Shift E

Figure 5.1 Using Word to track changes

Tools>Options>
Spelling &
Grammar

document. In Figure 5.1, the spell and grammar check have been turned off, so that they do not distract from the mark-up, or tell students in advance where there are errors. Tracking changes in this way allows both the original and the edited version to be seen simultaneously to facilitate discussion.

Pictures and clipart can be inserted into a document using the Insert menu on the top toolbar. Click on Insert>Picture and then select an option. This also allows you to insert WordArt. However, Word also has a Draw toolbar, which gives these options, plus many others. Figure 5.2 shows the Draw toolbar together with a few examples of what can be done using the Draw options.

If you cannot see a toolbar with Draw on the left-hand end (probably just above the Windows taskbar at the bottom of the screen), right click on any toolbar. A pop-up menu will open which gives you the option to open any other toolbar – select the Draw toolbar. Wherever the Draw toolbar opens, it can be moved to the top, bottom or either side of the screen as convenient by left clicking just to the left of Draw and then dragging the toolbar.

Figure 5.2 shows what some of the icons on the Draw toolbar do; to find out what other icons do, hover the mouse above them. Some allow different shapes to be inserted, while AutoShapes gives many different shape options and a free-hand pen. There are icons that connect to WordArt, clipart and picture files. The Insert Diagram or Organisation icon enables you to add flow-charts and other charts to your document. Other icons allow the colour and thickness of lines to be changed, and shapes to be filled with colour.

Insert>Text Box

Format Text Box or
Picture>
Layout

Text can be inserted onto drawings if it is typed into a Text Box. When text is put on top of an image, you may find, however, that it keeps moving away from where you want it to be. This may also happen if two images are placed next to each other. Experimenting with the Text Wrapping will enable you to change the layout of images and text and should solve problems of things moving of their own accord. In Line with Text is the option

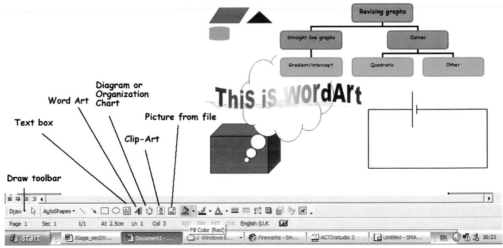

Figure 5.2 Draw toolbar

to choose if you want an image to appear next to text, and In Front of Text if you want an image on top of text. If a text box or image seems to disappear completely, use Ctrl Z or Undo to put it back where it was, then Draw>Order to bring it to the front.

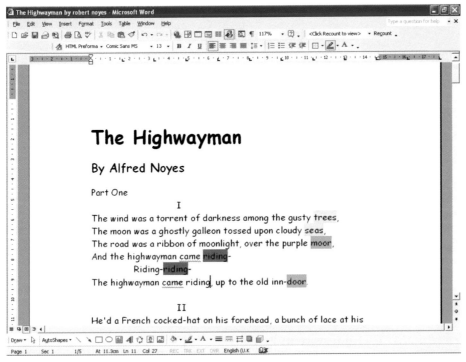

Figure 5.3

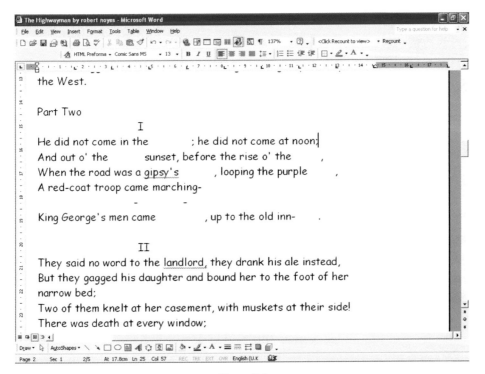

Figure 5.4

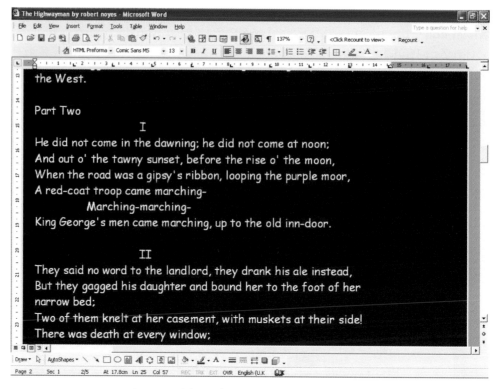

Figure 5.5 'The Highwayman' with text highlighted

Another useful feature in Word is the Highlight tool. With this turned on, individual words can be highlighted by pointing at them and double-clicking, or phrases and sections can be marked by running the cursor over them with your finger held down. In this extract from 'The Highwayman' by Robert Noyes, the rhyming scheme has been highlighted using different colours and the repetition picked out (Figures 5.3–5.5).

PowerPoint

PowerPoint is an extremely useful tool for anyone using an IWB, since slides can incorporate text, pictures, graphs, tables, sounds and video. Slides can also be annotated during a presentation with a freehand pen available in the PowerPoint software, which could be useful to those using just a data projector. There is not nearly as much choice of pen colour as with IWB annotation tools, however, and the pen width cannot be changed. These annotations cannot be saved either. A wide range of special effects can be used to animate a presentation. Some ideas for using these to create lesson materials are described in Chapter 7.

When preparing a PowerPoint presentation, it is a good idea to start by setting up a master for the slides, called the Slide Master, which can be found from View>Master>Slide Master. This allows text formatting to be chosen at the start, or an image to be added to all slides, so that all your slides show the chosen scheme.

A Design Template can be added to slides by clicking on Format>Apply Design, providing a range of designs which will give your slides a particular look or style.

You can set up a colour scheme for all your slides, using Slide Design. You will be offered a few colour schemes, which can be customised by clicking on Custom, and changing the colours in each of the boxes. To see what a colour scheme looks like, click on Preview to see it on the current slide. When you are happy with your design, click on Apply to All to put it onto all your slides. The colour and texture of the background can be changed separately by clicking on Format>Background on the top toolbar. Click on the right-hand arrow by the colour bar below your colour scheme – you will see your current colours displayed, plus the options More Colours and Fill Effects. Fill Effects allows you to choose a textured or patterned background or a picture.

Format>Slide Design

Once you have decided on your design, colour scheme, fonts, and so on, it is time to create a slide . You will be offered a choice of format for the slide – do you want a heading and bullet points, pictures only, text and pictures? Drawings can also be made on PowerPoint slides using the Drawing toolbar, which is the same as that in Word (p.44).

Insert>New Slide
Ctrl M

PowerPoint opens in Slide view in which slides can be created and edited. To display the presentation, use the View menu or the Slideshow icon just above the Start button. To run the display, click the mouse or tap on the screen with the pen/finger. Clicking or tapping on the screen again moves the presentation on to the next slide. To return to the previous slide use the 'up' arrow on the keyboard. To navigate elsewhere in the presentation, follow the Slide Navigation instructions in the margin to obtain a menu arrow in the bottom left of the screen. Clicking on this will give you a range of options that include slide navigation. This menu also includes the PowerPoint annotation pen. The 'Esc' (escape) key can be used to return to Slide view from Slideshow view.

View>Slideshow

Slide number (if known)>ENTER
or
'A' or '=' or mouse to bottom left of screen> click on arrow

When giving a presentation, you may want to show bullet points or pictures on a slide sequentially, rather than all at once. To do this, go to Slide Show on the top toolbar and select Animation Schemes or Custom Animation. Depending on which version of PowerPoint you are using, you will be given a new menu or a box which allows you to select from different ways in which material can be displayed. There is a wide range of options, and you will need to experiment with them to find out what they do. Using animations in classroom resources is discussed further in Chapter 7, and the effects used can be seen and edited in the files on the CD. Once you have selected an effect you have the opportunity to accompany it with a sound of some kind and/or have the text dim when a new bullet point is shown. PowerPoint contains a library of sounds and videos which can be accessed from the top toolbar using Insert>Movies and Sounds. You can also use this to access sound and video files of your own or to record a new sound file.

In many types of IWB software you can save annotations made on a PowerPoint slide using the annotation tools to a flipchart/notebook or onto the PowerPoint slide. If you do nothing the annotations will disappear when you continue with the presentation and you will not be able to restore them. To find out how to save annotations for a given IWB, see the specific details for that software in Chapter 6.

It is comparatively easy to add images to a PowerPoint presentation, and even to create photo albums of sets of images. As text boxes, speech bubbles and WordArt can also be inserted in a similar way, you can quickly create a shared class resource that can also be printed out for pupils to have individual copies.

In PowerPoint, a lot of its functions can be found in the 'Insert' menu, including New Slide, Text Box and, under the 'Picture' heading, ClipArt, WordArt and Autoshape. As you can see, just through this one menu you can add a slide and put and image and caption on it.

Also under the Picture heading is New Photo Album. One use for this could be to create a record of a field trip. The images need to be in electronic format, but these can either be from a digital camera or from a standard film developed onto a CD. In the example below, a year class visited the Thames Barrier as part of their geography studies on 'Rivers and Flooding'. They used a digital camera to photograph the barrier and also the surrounding area to consider how its nature was changing. These were then inserted into a PowerPoint presentation to use on the whiteboard by following Insert>Picture>New Photo Album (Figure 5.6). From here the user found the folder where the photos were, selected the ones to use (individual photos can be selected by holding down the Ctrl key while single-clicking on each one) then clicked the Insert button. The selected images were then ordered using the up and down buttons and the format – between one and four to a page – chosen. When the Create button was clicked the album was automatically made complete with a title page.

The different layouts, from one to four images a slide, with or without titles, allow you to place images next to each other for comparison or to group them thematically. If it doesn't look quite as you want you can simply use cut-and-paste methods to rearrange them between the slides.

Another way to use PowerPoint is to work with the slides in Normal View creating a presentation with the whole class, then running it in Slide Show View to see the results. This works because only text and graphics on the slide itself will be viewed. Anything placed in the grey area around it will remain unseen. In the example in Figure 5.7, labels for the key features of the barrier and the surrounding area have been created and can be dragged into place on the photo during a whole-class discussion.

Anything on the grey area will not be shown when the presentation is run. Only when the labels have been dragged onto the slide will they be visible in the presentation itself (Figure 5.8). In this way the class can discuss the key points of the image, place them on the photo, then view it completed with the labels in place.

PowerPoint also has a number of different formats for printing, from one slide per page to nine per page. As well as providing every pupil with a record this could

Figure 5.6 Creating a Photo Album in PowerPoint

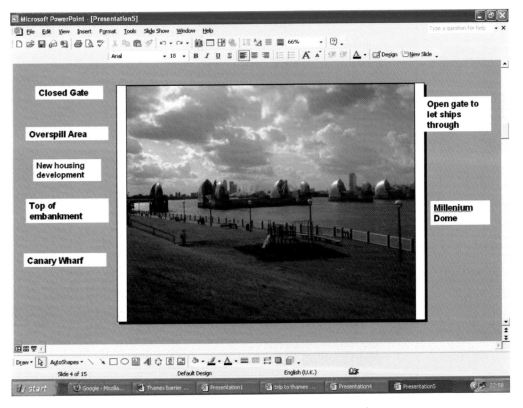

Figure 5.7 Slide with labels to be positioned

Figure 5.8 Slide with labels in place

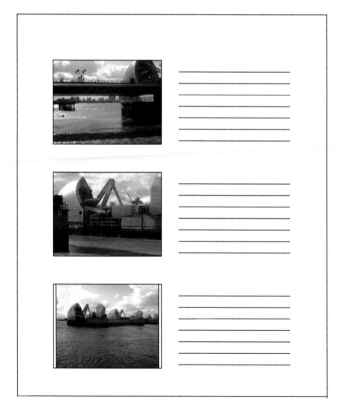

Figure 5.9 Three slides to a page

also be used for homework. In the example in Figure 5.9, pupils could write a short paragraph beside each photo about how the barrier works.

Using these printing options can also create other formats for publications. Six slides to a page appears similar to a comic strip or photo story. Posed photos of pupils or pieces of clipart can be used with speech bubbles to create conversations or enliven play scripts in English, for instance.

PowerPoint presentations can also be linked directly to the internet by using hyperlinks. First, select an object – an image, a text box or a selected piece of writing – and from the Insert menu choose Hyperlink. This will then give you the option of linking to another slide, a document on your computer or a website. If the latter, you can first open the site then highlight its address and copy and paste it into the Address box in the Hyperlink dialog box.

Finally, PowerPoint presentations also have the capacity to loop, that is to run continuously. This means that once a task has been explained through a presentation it can be left running as an ongoing reminder to pupils about the content of the lesson and the task they are engaged in.

Excel

Excel provides spreadsheets that can be used to show tabulated data, perform calculations and display graphs. Spreadsheets can be formatted to display tabulated data, then viewed full-screen, providing useful resources for many different topics. For example, the Periodic Table shown in Figure 5.10 is a spreadsheet which has been formatted to display the data and shown in Full Screen view for maximum impact.

Using graphs to illustrate data is useful in many curriculum areas as well as maths, and Excel can help you produce perfect graphs instantly in the classroom. There is a template in the resources on the CD (Figure 5.11 *Graphs_template.xls*) which will enable you to produce bar charts and pie charts on demand to record the results of a class vote or the answers given to multiple-choice questions if you do not have a voting system available (details on how to edit this and other resources are available on the CD in *Notes_on_resources.doc*). It is also very straightforward to produce a graph from scratch.

To format a spreadsheet, use Ctrl A on the keyboard to select all the cells, then proceed with the formatting. There are icons for setting background colour, font colour, font type and size on the toolbar, or the Format menus can be used for this.

To produce your own graph, select the data on the spreadsheet to be graphed, then click on the Chart Wizard icon on the top toolbar. This will give a dialogue box from which you can choose the type of graph you want. The Wizard will take you through the steps to produce a labelled

Background colour

Format>Cells> Patterns

Font Colour

Format>Cells> Font

Font type

Arial

Format>Cells> Font

Font size

16

Format>Cells> Font

Insert>Chart

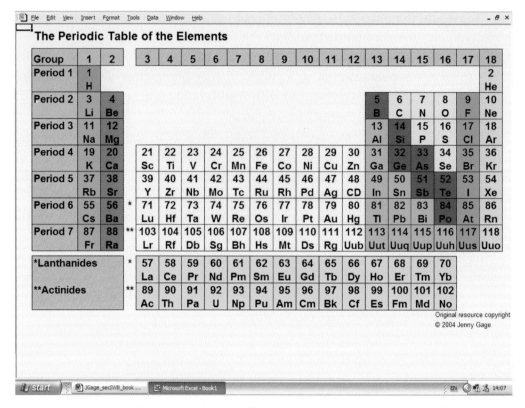

Figure 5.10 Using a spreadsheet to display tabulated data (Periodic_Table.xls)

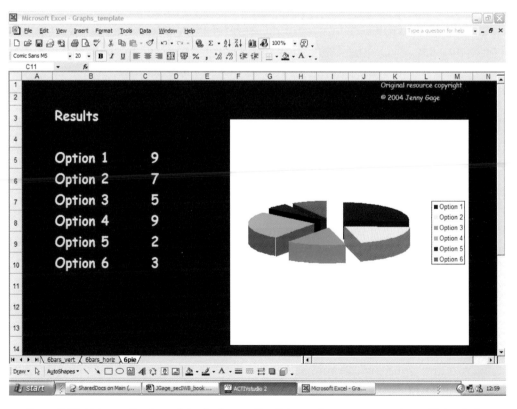

Figure 5.11 Using an Excel graph to display results of class votes or responses to multiple-choice questions (Graphs_template.xls)

graph. If the finished result is not to your liking you can format your graph by right-clicking on it. You can also format any area of the graph or the axes by right-clicking. This enables the default scales, fonts and colours to be changed.

It is possible to display a graph alongside the figures that produced it by choosing the As an object in Sheet# option as the wizard finishes. In this way the effect of any change in values is immediately shown on the graph. In Figure 5.12 the expression $y = x^2 - 6$ has produced a parabolic curve. The value of x is shown in column B and the value of y in column C. To create the graph the two sets of numbers were highlighted, then a Scatter Graph chosen from the selection in the wizard. When this was completed, the trendline was not shown. This was added by pointing at one of the plot marks, right-clicking and selecting Add Trendline from the options list.

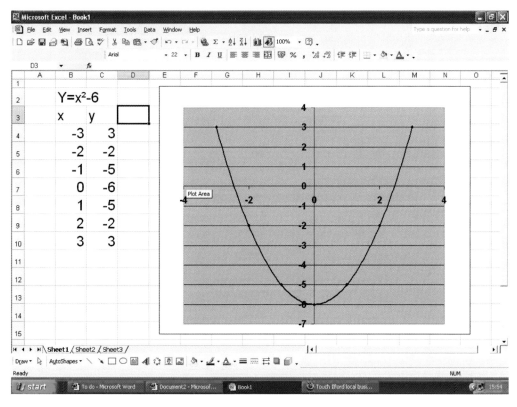

Figure 5.12 Graphing an equation

The figures have been generated using formulae so that by changing the value of cell B4 all the other cells will change too. This was done by putting the formula = b4 + 1 in cell B5 then copying this down into the cells below by dragging on the corner of the cell.

The formula for y in cell C4 is $= (B4 \times B4) + 6$. This is also copied into the following cells by dragging on the bottom corner of C4. Excel here has used relative cell references, meaning that it has automatically changed the formulae down the column. So cell B9 will contain the formula = B8 + 1 and cell C9 will have $= (B9 \times B9) + 6$ in it.

By using formulae in this way, when we change the value of cell B4 all the others will change automatically, as will the line graph. In Figure 5.13 the value of x has been changed to −5.

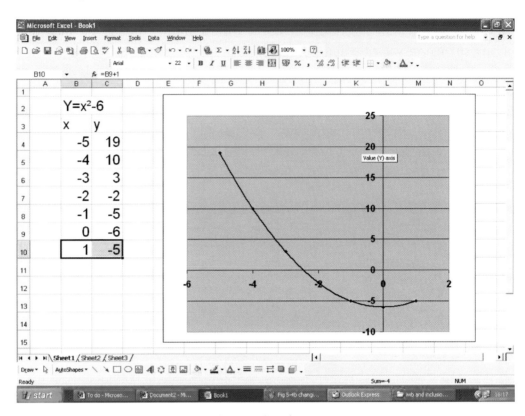

Figure 5.13 Changing the values in an equation

In order to get a symmetrical parabolic curve, an extra three lines will need to be added to the table. This can be done by highlighting the two cells as shown, picking up the lower right-hand corner and dragging down. The relevant formulae will simply be copied down.

Excel can also be used to provide ranges of numbers or random numbers so that spreadsheets can be used many times, giving students practice at arithmetic, interpreting graphs, estimating angles, and so on. To add a 'slider' (either with arrows to click or a sliding scale to change the number provided) to a spreadsheet, click on View>Toolbar>Forms. This will produce a floating toolbar which includes two types of slider. Right-clicking allows the slider to be repositioned or resized. Right-click and select Format control to set values for the slider and the cell where the value will appear.

To produce a random number between two values, a and b, type $=INT(RAND()*(a-b)+b)$ into a cell. Excel recognises that it is being asked to work out a formula by the initial = sign. INT gives the integer part of the following number, and RAND asks Excel for a random number, which will be greater than or equal to zero and less than 1. The values of a and b are used to scale the random number provided by Excel.

For example, if we want a random number between a minimum of −10 and a maximum of 10, then we need to put $a=11$ (not 10) and $b= −10$ into the formula, giving $=INT(RAND()*(11 − −10)+ −10)$. Now suppose Excel provides the random number 0.97823. The $*(11 − −10)$ in the formula multiplies this random number by 21 to give 20.54283. Adding −10 to this gives 10.54283, which has integer part 10, and so 10 will be displayed in the cell. Ten is the highest number that can be displayed with this formula, because RAND does not actually give 1 as a random number. The highest number it will give is 0.9999... Multiplying this by 21, then adding negative 10, gives 10.999..., and so the highest integer which can be produced is, in fact, 10. The lowest integer which can be produced by this formula is −10, since RAND can give 0 for the initial random number.

Several of the Excel classroom resources supplied on the accompanying CD use sliders or random numbers: these can all be edited by changing the upper and lower limits of the numbers that can be produced.

Paint

Many resources benefit from having pictures to illustrate them. These might be digital photos, clipart or pictures obtained from the internet. However, it is not always best to use pictures in their original form. Digital photos are often very big files, with areas that add nothing to the main content of the photo. There are many different software packages for editing photos and pictures, and if you have a digital camera you may have such a package. If not, Microsoft Paint, which is normally available in Windows, is quite adequate for basic editing and can also be used to create images and graphics from scratch.

Paint can be found from the Start button in Programs>Accessories>Paint. If you are unfamiliar with it, start by opening a new document in Paint. The top toolbar gives menus similar to those found in Word. However, there is also a left-hand, vertical toolbar containing icons specific to drawing packages, as shown in Figure 5.14.

Figure 5.14 shows the toolbars and icons in Paint, together with the names of the icons. Most are self-explanatory, and a little experimentation will show what they do. The Rectangle tool can be used to create a square by holding down the Shift key, and similarly the Ellipse tool can be used for a circle.

If the drawing canvas that appears on opening a new document is not the right size, there are 'handles' (faint grey marks – the cursor will change to a double-headed arrow when it is in the right place) on the bottom right corner and the right and bottom sides that can be used to change the size of the canvas. If the image is the wrong size, or the wrong orientation, this can be changed using the Image menu on the top toolbar. This is often useful for digital photos that may be very large or turned sideways. To crop a picture, select the area you want with one of the Select tools from the left-hand icons. You can then either copy and paste it into a new canvas or drag it away from the background to the

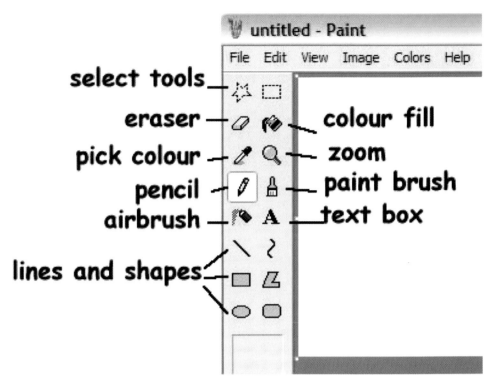

Figure 5.14 Toolbars in Paint

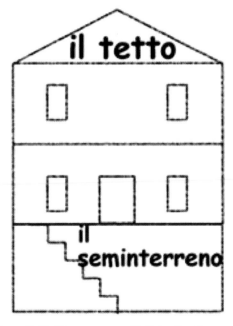

Figure 5.15 Diagram created in Paint (La_Casa.ppt)

top left of the canvas. Moving the handles in will then remove the unwanted background.

Paint can be used to create diagrams and images from scratch, as well as to edit existing images. For example, Figure 5.15 shows a diagram of a house, used in a

PowerPoint resource on the CD for stimulating conversation in Italian. Diagrams like this just require the Straight line, Rectangle and Text tools.

A more complicated image is shown in Figure 5.16. This was created mainly with the Pencil and Fill tools. The Ellipse tool (with the Shift key held down) was used to form a yellow filled circle, then petals in different colours drawn with the Pencil tool. The Colour menu allows a full-colour spectrum to be used. The petal shapes were filled with colour, then individual petals selected with the Freeform Select tool (which looks like a star) copied and pasted back onto the page. These were then rotated through 90 degrees (Image>Flip/Rotate). Final effects were achieved with the Airbrush tool. The background colour was produced with the Fill tool. At any stage, if the preceding operation did not give the required result, Undo or Ctrl Z was used to remove it.

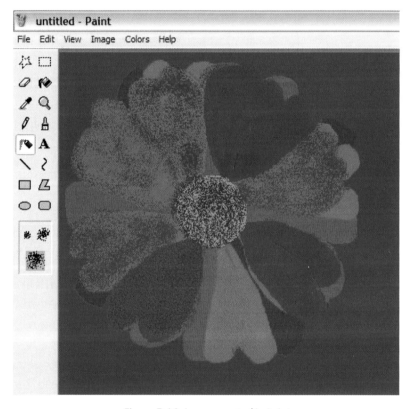

Figure 5.16 Image created in Paint

CHAPTER 6

Using Interactive Whiteboard software

Every IWB has its own software that can be used to great effect in producing classroom resources. This is what makes an IWB different from simply using a data projector and a computer – because IWB software is dynamic and interactive. Three different types of IWB software are discussed here: the SMARTBoard notebook, the ACTIVstudio2 flipchart produced by Promethean and the StarBoard flipchart produced by Hitachi.

SMARTBoard notebook

Getting started

The main things you will probably want to do to start with are to access a new page, insert freehand or typed text or a picture and navigate round pages you have created, then save and retrieve your document. Opening up the software will provide a new notebook; a new or existing notebook can also be opened in place of the current open notebook using icons on the top toolbar. During preparation you may find it useful to use standard Windows keyboard shortcuts for common operations (see pp.42–3).

When a new notebook page is opened, it will be white by default. You can change this through the Format menu (select Background Colour) or by right-clicking on the page. Right-clicking also gives options to Paste an object from the Windows clipboard to the page, to Select All objects on a page and to Clear Page.

Figure 6.1 shows the menu bar and toolbar on a SMARTBoard notebook. At the top are the drop-down menus and below them is the toolbar, which can also be dragged to the bottom of the screen for easy access,

New notebook

File>New
CtrlN
Opening a notebook

File>Open
Ctrl O

Page colour
Right-click>Set Background Color
Format> Background Color
Select all
Right-click>Select all
Edit>Select all
Ctrl A
Paste

Right-click>Paste
Edit>Paste
Ctrl V

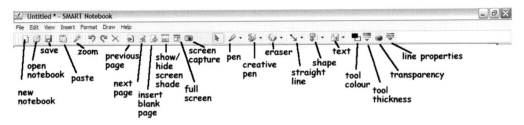

Figure 6.1 SMARTBoard toolbar

showing various shortcut icons. These include icons to give a new page, and to move to the previous or next page.

At the side of the notebook page is the Sidebar, with tabs for Page Sorter View, the Gallery and Attachments. These can be placed either to the left or the right of the page – to move them from one side to the other, click the arrow below the Attachments tab. Selecting Auto-Hide Sidebar in the top View menu allows you to hide this bar, except the tabs, simply by clicking in the page area. Page Sorter View shows all the pages in the current notebook, and can be used to change the order of pages, clear a page, insert a blank page or to duplicate or delete a page. To edit pages, click on the thumbnail image of the page, then on the arrow at the top right to access a menu of options. To change the order of pages, drag them to the required position. Figure 6.2 shows Page Sorter View and the page menu. Below the Page Sorter tab can be seen the Gallery tab which gives access to the page templates, lesson resources, clipart and Flash files available in the SMARTBoard

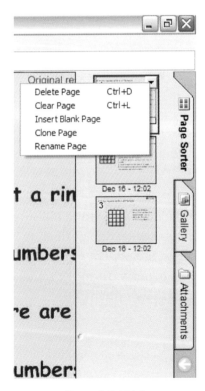

Figure 6.2 Sidebar

software, and the Attachments tab, through which other files, including sound and video, can be attached to a notebook.

The floating tools

The floating tools can be used with any application, not just with notebooks. They
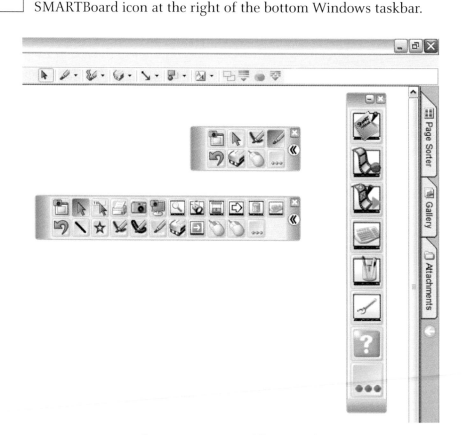
include the annotation tools, the ScreenCapture, ScreenShade and Spotlight tools. If they do not open automatically when the computer is connected to a SMARTBoard, they can be accessed by right-clicking on the SMARTBoard icon at the right of the bottom Windows taskbar.

SMARTBoard
icon

Figure 6.3 SMARTBoard floating tools

Figure 6.3 shows the default floating tools (top set of floating horizontal tools) and an enlarged collection of floating tools (lower set of floating horizontal tools). These are shown together here for illustration – they will not appear simultaneously. To add or remove tools, use the Customize Tool icon . The default tools contain:

Customize
Tools

◉ Area Capture

◉ Select arrow

◉ Pen

- ⦿ Highlighter

- ⦿ Undo/Redo

- ⦿ Eraser

- ⦿ Right-click

- ⦿ Customize

You may wish to add to these the Magnifier, Spotlight and ScreenShade tools. Depending on your curriculum area, the simple calculator (but note that this is not a scientific calculator, and it does not observe the correct order of operations) and keyboard might also be useful. The keyboard has various options, including a normal 'qwerty' keyboard and a number pad. It can be set to recognise handwriting and to give a verbal output of anything input via the keyboard.

One of the extra tools that can be added to the floating tools is the Start Centre. Clicking on this produces the vertical set of floating tools in Figure 6.3. These icons provide:

Start Center

- ⦿ new notebook

- ⦿ video/sound recorder

- ⦿ video/sound player

- ⦿ keyboard

- ⦿ Floating Tools

- ⦿ Control Panel (which includes the Pen Tray Settings to set default pen tray options)

- ⦿ Help

- ⦿ Customize Start Centre

To start annotating, click on the tool you wish to use. While the annotation tools are active, the document being annotated is not active, and vice versa. For example, if the annotation tools are used to edit a passage in Word, Word itself will be inactive and changes cannot be made to the passage in Word. To stop annotating so that the other document can be edited, click on the Select arrow on the floating tools. This will make the annotation layer disappear and the other document will become active again.

Annotations on a notebook page will be saved automatically when the notebook is saved. It is also possible to save annotations over other applications, such as Word, Excel or PowerPoint. Lifting a pen from the tray makes a floating toolbar appear that contains options allowing you to save your annotations either to a notebook page, or as an object in the application currently open. Such objects can then be edited using the Microsoft Draw editing toolbar. Alternatively, the Screen Capture tool (see p.67) can be used to copy any annotations either to a notebook or to the Windows clipboard. From the clipboard, these can be pasted into any application.

The pen tray and handwriting recognition

In addition to the floating tools, there are four pens in the pen tray automatically linked to a particular colour. However, the colour, width and even the function of these pens can be changed by removing the pen from the tray, then setting the colour/width/transparency required on the appropriate tool in the floating tools. A pen can be used as a Creative Pen, as a Highlighter or as an Eraser. To erase free-hand writing or drawing, use the eraser from the pen tray.

Handwriting can be converted to typed text. To do this, select the handwriting, then click on the menu arrow in the top right corner of the selection box, as in Figure 6.4.

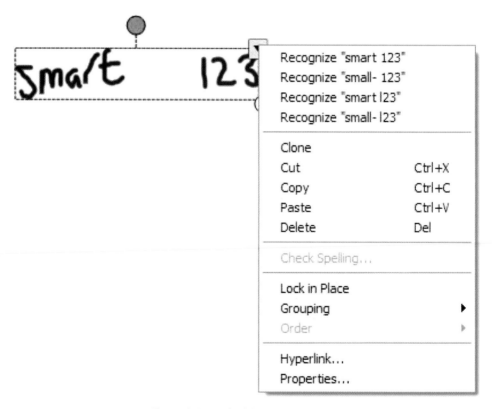

Figure 6.4 Handwriting recognition

In Figure 6.4, various options for the alphabetic and numeric handwritten words/numbers are given. Clicking on the desired option will convert the hand-writing to text that can then be edited if necessary. This is particularly useful when brainstorming in class, as ideas can be written up as they occur, then converted to text for printed notes later.

Preparing a notebook without the board

SMARTBoard software can be used on a computer without the board attached, which is useful for preparation. The floating tools cannot be used without the board, but everything else is accessible.

To insert freehand writing in preparation, use the pen tool which can be accessed either by using the Pen icon on the toolbar, or from the Draw>Pen menu. Freehand writing can be removed with the Eraser tool or by pulling a selection box around it (first choose the Select icon on the toolbar) and then using the Delete key on the keyboard. Alternatively, use Ctrl Z or the Undo icon to remove the last action.

To insert typed text, make sure none of the pen or shape tools are selected, and then simply start typing anywhere on a notebook page. Text can be moved to a better position by dragging it; to change the layout of text, such as where line breaks occur, double-click on it to edit and put in line breaks through the keyboard. To change the font size, type or colour of text, either double-click to edit or single-click and use Properties from the drop-down menu, accessed from the arrow at the top right.

Items on a flipchart page, such as text, shapes or pictures, can be moved, resized and rotated. Tap on a piece of text or a picture. You will see a dotted line around the object with a white circle at the bottom right and a green circle above the top middle of it. The object can be moved by dragging it, or to resize it, pull the white circle at the bottom right. This can be pulled diagonally which maintains the height:width ratio, or vertically or horizontally, which distorts it. Resizing a text box will affect the font size, not the layout of the text. The green circle above a selected object allows rotation in either direction.

When text or objects are selected, in addition to the resizing and rotation handles, an arrow will appear at the top right. Clicking on this gives a drop-down menu containing options to Clone, Cut, Copy, Paste and Delete the text or object. It also includes options to lock the object in place on the page, to group items together or to change their order, so that one object appears above another. The Properties option allows editing of colour, transparency and text or line style to be changed.

Adding pictures

To insert a picture from the clipart included in the SMARTBoard software, go to the Gallery and select the category you want. The Gallery contains a huge range of lesson resources, pictures, page templates and Flash files, and it is well worth browsing through all the categories to see what is available, not just your own curriculum area. This is where you can access different page backgrounds and grids, including graph paper, music paper, lined paper and a host of others. Page backgrounds can be distinguished by the folded top-right corner and Flash files by the 'f' symbol on them. To use any of the resources, simply drag them onto the page. Selecting an object then provides the resizing and rotation handles and the drop-down menu for further options. To remove a page background, use the Undo icon or Ctrl Z.

To insert a photo or a picture directly from a Scanner, go to Insert>Picture from Scanner. To insert a photo or picture you already have on your computer, choose Insert>Clipart, and instead of selecting from the folders shown, navigate up through the folders to the one you want. In each case, once you have the picture you want, click on Open. If you find that your picture is too big for the page, use the Extend Page link at the bottom of the page until you can see the bottom of the picture. Then tap on the picture to select it, and use the bottom right-hand corner circle to pull it to the size you want. You can also drag the picture to place it where you want. To remove a picture, or any other object, select it and then press the Delete icon or use the keyboard.

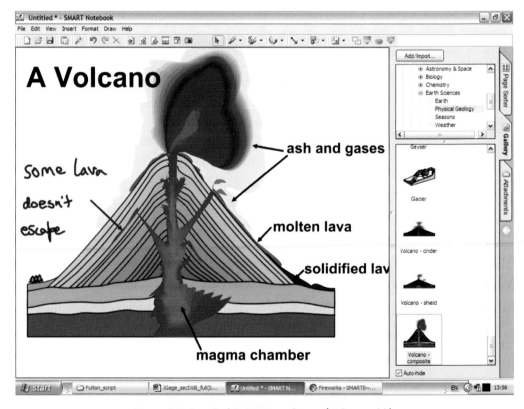

Figure 6.5 A typical SMARTBoard page (Volcano.xbk)

Figure 6.5 shows a new page created with typed text and handwritten annotation, arrows created with the straight-line tool and a picture from the SMARTBoard Gallery. At the bottom of the screen, the other applications open are displayed on the taskbar, so that navigating from one application to another is just a matter of tapping on these tabs. On the right, the Gallery is open, showing a selection of clipart resources from the Earth Sciences section.

Attaching files and hyperlinks

Hyperlinks and shortcuts to other files or to web pages can be inserted into a notebook via the Attachments tab on the Sidebar. This enables you to link quickly to other resources during a lesson, thus maintaining pace. Clicking on the Attachments tab and then on the Insert button gives options to insert a file, a short-cut to a file or a hyperlink to a web page. Using the Attachments tab to insert a hyperlink puts the link in the Attachments View, and alternative text can be chosen if desired. Another option is to use the Insert menu for hyperlinks – this displays the hyperlink as text on the page, but the text must then show the URL of the web page.

The SMARTBoard recorder

SMARTBoard software includes a recorder that can be used to record a video file of anything done on the SMARTBoard (whether in a notebook or in any other application). Sound can also be recorded to accompany the video recording if a microphone is available. The video recorder and player can be accessed through the Start Centre or through the SMARTBoard icon on the bottom right of the Windows taskbar. This facility is very useful where students might want to watch a sequence of annotations, with or without a voice-over, more than once, or where a record of students' work needs to be kept.

Video recorder

Video player

Other menu options

The File menu contains save and print options as in Word and similar applications. A page can be saved as a template using File>Save Page as Template, which saves it as an *.xbt* file either to the My Content folder of the Gallery or to another location. Saving it to the Gallery makes it easy to access for future use. Such a template might contain background colours and/or objects such as sets of axes or maps, as in Figure 6.6. Templates can then be printed out as worksheets for student use. There is also an option to export a page as a pdf, html or image file.

The Edit menu contains options for deleting pages, copying and pasting, just as in Word. A quick way to copy and paste objects from or to another application is to drag them via the Windows (bottom) taskbar. To remove an object from its current location (cut), select it and drag it down to the appropriate tab on the taskbar. This will open that application and paste the object into it. To copy the object, rather than removing it from its current location, first hold down the

Figure 6.6 Background template (Graphs_background.xbt)

Ctrl key. The Edit menu also contains a Spelling Check option (or use F7 as a keyboard shortcut).

Options available in the View menu include:

- ⊙ Whiteboard

- ⊙ Page Sorter

- ⊙ Attachments Views (also accessible from the Sidebar)

- ⊙ Next Page

- ⊙ Previous Page

- ⊙ Screen Capture

- ⊙ Screen Shade

- ⊙ Full Screen

View>Next Page
Page down

View>Previous Page
Page up

View>Screen Capture Toolbar

View>Screen Shade

View>Full Screen
Alt Enter

View>Zoom

Full Screen is useful where you want to display a presentation without the distraction of the toolbars, or where you need a bit more space to show all of a page, as it removes the toolbars and page sorter from around the whiteboard. To return to Whiteboard view, just tap on the icon again or use the 'Esc' key on the keyboard. Click on Show/Hide Screen Shade to put a screen over the page, which can be pulled up and down or from side to side to hide and reveal objects on a page, as you might do with a piece of paper over an overhead projector transparency. Tap it again to remove the screen.

The 'camera' icon on the toolbar and on the floating tools, corresponding to View>ScreenCapture, is extremely useful. You can use this tool either in a notebook or in any other application you are using, including internet pages, which makes it an easy way to copy pictures and text. Selecting ScreenCapture produces a floating toolbar, with options of Area, Window, Screen and a box to select for Save Pictures to a New Page. Selecting this box will mean your snapshot is printed on a new page; not selecting it will mean that it is printed on the current page.

Area enables you to draw out the area you wish to copy. This option was used to copy a set of axes on graph paper onto a new page, which was then copied and pasted four times to produce the template shown in Figure 6.6. Selecting Window means the whole of the document you are working in will be copied, but not the toolbars around the outside of the active window. Selecting Screen means that the whole screen, including the toolbars, will be copied. There is also a ScreenCapture icon on the floating tools. This works in the same way, with options of Capture the Screen and Capture an Area. Both put the picture onto a new page of a notebook, however, without giving you the choice of putting it onto the current page.

The Insert menu allows you to insert a blank page, Flash files, clipart and pictures, and hyperlinks into your notebooks. A link can be made to a picture, a video or any other resource. The Insert>Picture option can be used to navigate to any file on the computer or to those in the Gallery.

The Format menu contains options for formatting text and for changing the thickness and colour of drawing objects through the Properties option. Background colour enables you to set the colour you want for your page. You can save favourite background colours as templates, so that they are quickly available, which is useful if the colour you want is not one of those in the colour chart. Once a page is set up, if you want to be sure that background material or text is not inadvertently moved, use Format>Lock Position. The transparency of objects and text can also be changed using the Format menu.

The Draw menu includes:

◉ Pen

◉ Creative Pen

◉ Eraser

◉ Line

◉ Shapes

◉ Text

These are all also displayed as icons on the top toolbar. Holding down the Shift key with Shapes gives squares, circles or shapes with equal sides; not holding it down means that rectangles, ellipses and irregular shapes can be drawn. The Draw menu also allows objects to be grouped together or ordered. Grouped objects can be resized or moved as a single object. Order allows you to decide which objects should be on top and which should be underneath, as well as enabling you to put certain objects into the background.

Last, but not least, is the Help menu. Help menus can be a mixed blessing – you have to know what the item you want is called. However, looking through the Index can be a way round this problem. You can use the more specific options to remind yourself how to do a particular operation, or use the overviews to find out more about what your software can do. The more you use the Help menu when you are stuck or have a question, the more familiar with its contents you will become.

ACTIVstudio2 flipchart

Getting started

Flipchart

A new flipchart with a white background (unless you change the default colour) will open when you open AS2 and then click the Flipchart icon on the floating toolbar. To change the background colour of a page, double-click the pen on the page to give the Page Edit toolbar, as in Figure 6.7.

Figure 6.7 Page Edit toolbar in AS2

Cut

Copy

Paste

Delete

Duplicate

The icon with a red 'tick' on it gives the Properties dialogue box. Select Appearance, and then click on the Page Colour square. This will open up a colour chart. For more colours, click on the square icon with three dots to open up a full colour spectrum.

The Page Edit toolbar also provides the following options:

⊙ Cut

⊙ Copy

⊙ Paste

◉ Delete

◉ Duplicate

Cut, Copy and Duplicate all put a copy of the page onto the clipboard. However, Cut removes it from its current position, Copy leaves it alone and gives the option to Paste it back as an image on the same page or as a new page, while Duplicate creates an immediate copy of the page. Delete removes it entirely.

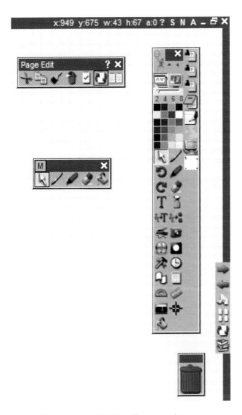

Figure 6.8 AS2 toolbars and icons

Figure 6.8 shows the toolbars and icons on a flipchart page. The icons at the far right of the page can be used for page navigation, and to create new pages. To see all the pages in the current flipchart, click on the Page Selector icon – the pages will appear on the right of the current page. Any page can be accessed by clicking on it here. To go back to viewing a single page, click the Page Selector icon again. Below the Page Selector icon is the Page Organiser. This view shows all the pages in the flipchart, and allows you to copy or delete pages or to change their order. Clicking on Return to page view at the bottom of this page will return you to the normal flipchart view. Page Reset takes a page back to the saved version. The Resource Library is described later (pp.75ff).

AS2 can be used on a computer without a board attached for preparation of resources although a watermark will be displayed across all

Next page

Previous page

Page selector

Page organiser

Page reset

Resource library

flipchart pages, but this will not show when the board is attached. Some tools, such as the handwriting recognition tool, will not work without a board, but most of the tools can be used so that full preparation can be done away from the board.

The floating toolbars

Promethean man

Unlike most other software, AS2 does not have a toolbar along the top allowing access to common menus or icons. Instead, it has several floating toolbars with icons giving access to various operations and resources (Figure 6.8). We have already looked at the Page Edit toolbar. Common operations, like saving and printing, are in a menu accessed from the Promethean man at the top of the floating tools.

If you open AS2 and then open a Word or PowerPoint document, or any other application, you will see the floating toolbar containing annotation tools that can be used over any application including internet sites. This toolbar can be moved by dragging, so that it is not in the way, or the scroll arrows can be used to roll it up when it is not in use.

The annotation tools include:

⊙ Undo

⊙ Redo

⊙ Pen

⊙ Highlighter

⊙ Eraser

⊙ Camera

⊙ Clear Screen

To start annotating, click on the tool you wish to use. While the annotation tools are active, the document being annotated is not active, and vice versa. For example, if the annotation tools are used to edit a passage in Word, Word itself will be inactive and changes cannot be made to the passage in Word. To stop annotating so that the other document can be edited, click on the Windows icon on the floating tools. This will make the annotation layer disappear, and the other document will become active again. To save any annotations, use the Camera tool and paste the snapshot into the original document or onto a flipchart page.

Windows

Annotations can also be saved with the original document if they are made through the ACTIVmarker. To select this, click on the Promethean Man, then ACTIVextras>ACTIVmarker. A small toolbox will appear which has a pen and highlighter tool. Annotations made with these will become part of the original document. If highlighting moves away from text in Word that it is supposed to cover, select it and then click the Text Wrapping icon on the Draw toolbar and choose In Front of Text. To stop annotating, click

Text wrapping

on the original document, or turn off the ACTIVmarker by clicking on the ACTIVmarker icon on the right of the bottom toolbar. This will restore the floating toolbar.

Clicking on the Promethean man on the floating toolbar gives a drop-down menu, from which the ACTIVmarker is obtained. Of the other choices available, Flipchart, Toolbox Customise and Help are probably the most important, initially. Flipchart gives further options for opening a new or existing flipchart, and for saving and printing a flipchart. At the bottom of the drop-down menu, you will see a list of the flipcharts you have used recently, which provides short-cuts to them. Toolbox Customise opens up all the toolboxes so that you can drag icons you want available all the time onto the floating toolbar. Toolbox Customise also allows you to decide how big you want the icons (and hence the floating toolbar) to be, and where you want it to be. Where a board is used by more than one person, each can save their own preferred settings and toolbox. Help menus can be a mixed blessing – you have to know what the item you want is called. However, looking through the Index can be a way round this problem. You can use the more specific options to remind yourself how to do a particular operation, or use the overviews to find out more about what your software can do. The more you use the Help menu when you are stuck or have a question, the more familiar with its contents you will become.

AS2 also has context-dependent Help. Right-clicking on a tool or icon will give details of the operation of that particular tool.

Another option in the main menu is Studio Settings. This opens a dialogue box through which you can specify everything from the default colour of your flipchart pages (Flipchart) to whether you want the Shape Recognition tool to fill shapes or not (Shape Recognition) or the on-screen keyboard to appear automatically whenever you open a text box (User Input). It is worth looking through what each of the settings does from time to time, and updating these as necessary.

Clicking once on an object (image or text) will select it. It will have resizing handles and can be dragged around the page. Double-clicking on an object gives another floating toolbar, the Object Edit toolbar. This toolbar has options for editing the object.

Figure 6.9 is a composite picture put together for illustration purposes to show the difference between the Object Edit toolbars for images and text: the toolbar above the text contains a 'T' icon not present on the toolbar above the image. This is used to edit text. In fact, images and text cannot be selected simultaneously with separate Object Edit toolbars. To select two or more objects at the same time drag a selection box round them; they will then act as

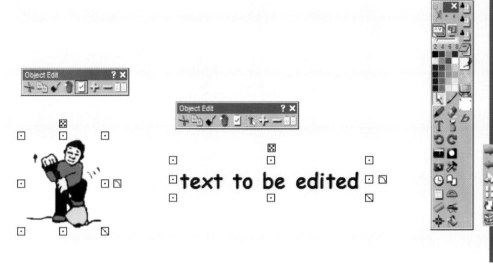

Figure 6.9 Edit object toolbar

Cut

Copy

Paste

Delete

Resize

Duplicate

Properties

a single object with a single Object Edit toolbar. For both objects and text, there are icons to:

⊙ Cut

⊙ Copy (to the clipboard)

⊙ Paste

⊙ Delete

⊙ Resize (will change the font size of text)

⊙ Duplicate (copy to the current page)

Both objects and text also have a Properties icon. Where two or more objects are selected, Properties>Identification allows them to be grouped, so that they can be moved or resized together, or ungrouped if they were previously grouped. Properties>Appearance allows you to change the order of objects – objects on a higher layer will appear on top of objects on a lower layer. Appearance also includes translucency, and the options to reflect or invert an image, or to give text a background colour or shading. Properties>Actions allows you to link objects to another page in a flipchart, or to another document or to a sound file, so that when they are tapped with the pen, they perform the given action.

A further range of options is available on another floating toolbar obtained by right-clicking on the page or on an object. This gives access to the pen, highlighter, eraser and Fill tools, and can be useful if you do not want the main floating toolbar visible on the screen. The 'M' icon in the corner (Figure 6.8) gives a drop-down menu, which includes Edit and Paste options. Edit leads to a further menu that gives another way to cut, copy, paste and delete. This menu also allows you to lock or unlock objects, bring them to the front or back of a layer, change the layer they are on and lock them to the background. The Paste menu shows what can be pasted (depending on what is on the clipboard) and allows you to select the object or text required.

Writing and drawing freehand

To write or draw freehand, select the pen icon on the floating toolbar, choose the colour and line width you want from the colour palette and width selector above the pen icon on the toolbar and then start writing or drawing. More colours can be made available on this toolbar, up to a maximum of 24, from the Promethean Man>Toolbox Customise>Colours. Right-clicking on one of the colour squares will open Select a Colour, with the bottom right icon with three dots on it giving access to a full colour spectrum. This can be used to customise the colours available.

Right-clicking on the pen icon will give a set of floating shapes which include:

◉ straight lines (vertical, horizontal and inclined)

◉ squares

◉ rectangles

◉ circles

◉ arrows

To remove freehand writing or drawing, actions can be undone one at a time with the Undo tool – the Redo tool reverses the Undo tool (these can both be found on the floating toolbar). Alternatively, there is an Eraser tool and a Clear tool. The eraser does not actually erase what is written, but puts a layer over it so that it is no longer visible. This layer can be removed with the Undo tool or moved aside, showing the original writing or drawing still visible on the page. The Clear tool gives options for what should be erased, from just freehand scribbles to all the objects on a page, or the entire page.

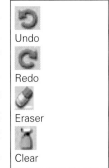

The Shape Recognition tool is extremely useful for converting freehand writing and shapes into something recognisable, although it can only be used with the board attached to the computer. Start by clicking on the Recognition Tool icon on the floating toolbox (if it is not there, go to Promethean Man>Toolbox Customise>Toolstore and drag it onto the toolbox). This will open up the Recognition Toolbar, which can be seen in the four images in Figure 6.10.

To convert handwriting to text, as in the two top images, select the alphabetic (ABC) or alphanumeric (ABC/123) icon on the bottom left of the toolbar, and make

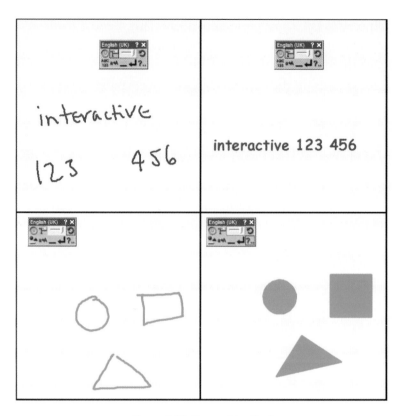

Figure 6.10 Recognition Tool

sure the Recognition Tool is turned on (its Start button should be green rather than red). Then just start writing. The slider allows you to set the interval between writing and recognition. The 'T' icon gives you options for setting the required font and other options allow lower-case letters to be recognised as capitals, or a space or carriage return to be inserted. The handwriting Recognition Tool recognises words in languages other than English, including French, German, Spanish and Italian.

To convert drawings into specific shapes (lower two images in Figure 6.10), select the shape icon on the lower left of the toolbar, and draw a shape. Shapes with a small gap will be completed, as well as those where the line returns to its starting point. You can choose whether shapes are filled or not (and with which colour) by selecting Promethean Man>Studio Settings>Shape Recognition. It may help to have a grid on the page for making shapes this way, as it is possible to select 'Snap to Grid' and 'Mask Grid', so that the grid does not show, but shapes are oriented to the grid. Double-click on the page to access the Page Edit toolbar to select grid options. To find a grid, click on the Resource Library icon at the bottom of the icons at the right of the page, then select Grids and drag the one you want onto the page (grids are discussed in more detail later in this section).

The Recognition Tools can be used to input text, numbers or shapes in other applications also. This means you could produce text for inclusion in Word, or put numbers into a spreadsheet, simply by handwriting on the document. The carriage return will operate as an ENTER key in Excel, and the space bar will give a space at the end of a sentence in Word. You need to turn off the Recognition Tool when it is not required, however, as it will override anything else you do, either in a flipchart or in any other application.

Inserting typed text

To insert typed text, click on the 'T' icon on the floating toolbar. This will give the Edit Text toolbar, which allows you to choose options for font type, colour, size and so on. Then just start typing on the flipchart page. The text can be moved by dragging it, or it can be edited by double clicking to bring up the Object Edit toolbar, then choosing the 'T' icon. The '+' and '−' icons on the Object Edit toolbar can be used to change font size if no other editing is required. Text can be removed by dragging it to the dustbin at the bottom right of the page, by selecting the dustbin icon in the Object Edit toolbar, or by using the Clear icon on the floating toolbar – Clear Objects will remove text and other objects on a page.

The on-screen keyboard can be set to appear automatically, or not, when the Text Tool is selected. To do this, click on Promethean Man>Studio Settings>User Input. Alternatively, a floating keyboard can be accessed through the Power Tools icon on the floating toolbar. On the keyboard, the Keyboard menu gives various options for the number of keys displayed and the layout. The Settings menu allows font type, size, colour, and so on, to be chosen.

Power Tools

Inserting images

Figure 6.11 shows a new page created with a background, images, typed text, arrows and a tickertape message from the AS2 resources. On the left is the Resource Library, which is currently open at Shared Images>Secondary> Geography>Industry. On the far right are the page icons, and next to them the floating toolbar. To the left, and down, there is the Pen Toolbar, with straight lines, shapes, arrows, and so on. Below the floating toolbar is the dustbin, into which any object no longer wanted on the page can be dragged to delete it. The images and text can be dragged to the correct position on the map, then linked with the Arrow tool. The tickertape ('No homework tonight') can be set to give any message, and the speed with which it moves across the screen can be regulated.

You can access a wealth of resources by clicking on the Resource Library icon at the bottom of the fixed icons on the far right of the page. The Resource Library toolbar can be moved to a convenient position on the page, and scrolled up when not needed. It gives options for choosing backgrounds, grids, images and much else. To select an item from the Resource Library, just drag it onto the page. To remove it, drag it into the dustbin, or select it and press Delete on the keyboard. Objects can be resized by selecting them, then dragging on the resizing handles. Double-clicking on an object will open the

Resource Library

Figure 6.11 Creating a typical page in AS2 (UK_map2.flp)

Object Edit toolbar. At the bottom of the Resource Library toolbar are options to give objects transparent or coloured backgrounds, and there is also a rubber-stamp tool. When this is selected it will produce further copies of the chosen item.

You can also make your own objects and save them in the Resource Library. At the top of the Resource Library toolbar are icons with two heads (Shared Resource Library) and with one head (My Resource Library). There is also a folder icon which allows you to navigate to other folders outside AS2. If you create an object that you wish to keep for future use, just open the folder you want to store it in – My Resource Library is designed specifically for this – then drag the object into it. You will be asked for a name for the object, and can then save it.

Grids and backgrounds

Page Edit>Snap to Grid

Page Edit>Grid Mask

The Grid and Background icons in the Resource Library open up menus with a wide range of backgrounds, including lined paper, squared and graph paper, music paper, maps, mazes, board games, and many others. A grid can be superimposed over another background. Grids and backgrounds can be edited by double-clicking on the page, so that the Page Edit toolbar opens. The Page Edit toolbar for a grid includes icons for Snap to Grid and Grid Mask. Snap to Grid means lines will snap to the lines and vertices of the grid, which is useful for drawing exact shapes, or aligning them. Mask Grid hides the grid but still allows Snap to Grid to operate.

You can also make your own backgrounds to save and use in future flipcharts. The easiest way to do this is to use the camera tool to make an image of your background (this should be the whole screen, although not any toolbars). Then drag it into the Image section of My Resource Library. You cannot drag backgrounds directly into the Backgrounds section, but can only put items here by saving them directly into the folder, for instance through Windows Explorer.

Special tools

An extremely useful icon to have on the floating toolbar is the Power Tools icon. Clicking on this provides a range of special tools on another floating toolbar. These include the:

- Ruler Tool

- Protractor Tool

- Dice Tool

- Fraction Creator (which can only be used when the board is attached)

- Calculator

- Keyboard

- Web Browser

- Tickertape Tool

- Flipchart Recorder

- Clock

The Ruler Tool gives the option of a ruler in centimetres or in inches. This can be resized by dragging on the resizing handles when it is selected. Clicking on the ruler gives '+' and '−' options. These increase or decrease the number of units shown on the ruler. The ruler can be dragged across the page and it can also be rotated by putting the pen on the scale so that a rotation symbol shows. When the ruler is rotated, it indicates what its angle of rotation is. Next in the Special Tools is a protractor. This gives the choice of a half (180-degree) or full (360-degree) protractor. Like the ruler, this can be dragged across the screen and rotated. It can be resized by dragging the resizing handles when it is selected.

The Calculator needs to be used with care as it is only a simple calculator, not a scientific calculator, and does not observe the correct order of operations. However, the calculator can be used over any application, not just on a flipchart.

Right-clicking on the calculator gives a choice of adult or child versions, plus the option of having the output pasted onto a flipchart page.

The Clock Tool can be used to set a timer for an activity. At the end of the time set, a sound can be made or an action, such as turning to a new flipchart page, carried out. The Flipchart Recorder enables you to record a series of actions on a flipchart page, for instance going through a calculation, so that it can be replayed as desired. Both these tools allow you to set up an activity and then leave the board to carry out actions by itself, freeing you to work with students.

Incorporating sounds

An easy way to start to use sounds is to use those in the Shared Resource Library>Shared Sounds, which include cheering, an alarm clock, a drum roll and an explosion. To link one of these to a page, drag it onto the page from the Resource Library, then click on it. If nothing happens, right-click on the page and select the 'M' icon to access the drop-down menu. If Enable Actions is not ticked, click on it. If this is not the problem, check that the computer has the sound turned up sufficiently.

A far greater range of sounds can be attached to objects. Double-click on the object to access the Object Edit toolbar. Click on Properties>Actions and click on the arrow at the right-hand end of the box at the bottom of the dialogue box. This will give Play Sound as one of the options. Once this is selected the dialogue box will give the option Set. Click on this to open the AS2 sound folders and choose the required sound, then close the dialogue box. Now when you move the pen across the object it will display a curved arrow, which indicates that the object carries a hyperlink. Clicking on the object will open the sound file. You can attach a sound file of your own in the same way, by navigating to the file.

Attaching files and hyperlinks

Any file on your system, including other applications, sounds and video, or a website, can be linked to a page or an object on a page. To make a link to an object, double-click to access the Object Edit toolbar, then select Properties>Actions>Open Document or File or Open Embedded Document or File. Choose Set and then enter the path and filename or URL, or use the Browse icon at the end of this box to find a file. Once a file is linked to an object, moving the pen over the object will show the hyperlink arrow, and clicking on the object will open the file. To make a link to another flipchart page, double-click an object, then select Object Properties>Actions from the Object Edit toolbar. Click on the arrow at the right of the box with 'Do nothing' in it and choose the action required, followed by Set.

To edit a link, right-click to get the 'M' icon. Click on this and de-select Enable Actions, remembering to select Enable Actions again when editing is complete. Embedding a document or file means it becomes part of the flipchart page, so that if you move the flipchart or the document or file, the link will still work. If the document or file is not embedded, then moving it or the flipchart will prevent the link operating.

This section is by no means an exhaustive description of all that can be done in AS2. However, it should provide sufficient information to get you started on producing resources. Use the Help menu and software overviews to explore the software further, or go to Promethean's website (see Appendix 1) for further ideas or help.

Hitachi StarBoard

One major difference between the StarBoard and all other boards is that it can also be used for PC-based video-conferencing. Discussion of this feature is, however, beyond the scope of this book.

Getting started

Opening the software brings up the StarBoard floating toolbar. All operations on the StarBoard are controlled through the menus accessible from the StarBoard icon at the bottom of the floating toolbar, or the icons on the toolbar. Frequently used icons can be dragged from the menus onto the floating toolbar, to save time during preparation or operation in the classroom.

Document>New blank page

To open a new flipchart, click on New blank page, which will give a new, white flipchart page. To change the background colour of a page, select the StarBoard icon at the bottom of the floating toolbar and then select Settings>Option Setting>View. This will give a dialogue box in which you can change the default page colour as required. To add pages, click on the New page icon on the floating toolbar. To navigate between pages, use the Next page and Previous page icons.

View>Next page

View>Previous page

View>Page List

To view all the pages in a flipchart, click on the Page List icon on the floating toolbar. This will show Captured Images and PC Screen. Clicking on Captured Images will show all the pages in the current flipchart. Clicking on PC Screen will return you to the computer desktop. Captured Images also gives the options to save and print a flipchart. Pages can be copied by selecting Capture and deleted by dragging them into the dustbin at the bottom-right corner of the dialogue box. The order of pages can be changed by moving them in this box.

The StarBoard can be used without a board attached for preparation of resources. Some tools, such as the handwriting recognition tool, will not work without a board, but most tools can be used so that full preparation can be done away from the board.

The floating toolbar

Unlike most other software, the StarBoard does not have a toolbar along the top allowing access to the menus. Instead it has a floating toolbar with icons giving access to various operations and resources, and access via the StarBoard icon at the bottom to the full range of menus available (Figure 6.12). If adding extra icons onto the toolbar makes it too large, smaller icons can be chosen and the toolbar folded, by using the Settings>Option Settings>Toolbar dialogue box. When not in immediate use, the top arrow on the floating tools can be used to scroll it down.

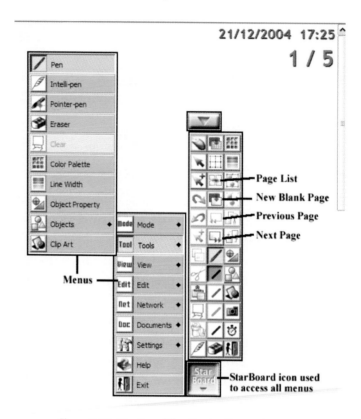

Figure 6.12 StarBoard floating toolbar and menus

The Help menu can be accessed from the StarBoard icon. If you open the StarBoard software, then open a Word or PowerPoint document, or any other application, you will see the floating toolbar containing annotation tools which can be used over any application, including websites. This toolbar can be moved to a convenient place on the screen by dragging the StarBoard icon. The annotation tools include a pen (which can be converted to a highlighter), the Undo and Redo tools and the Screen Capture tool. Help menus can be a mixed blessing – you have to know what the item you want is called. However, looking through the Index can be a way round this problem. You can use the more specific options to remind yourself how to do a particular operation, or use the overviews to find out more

Edit>Undo

Edit>Redo

Mode>
Accessories>
Screen Capture

about what your software can do. The more you use the Help menu when you are stuck or have a question, the more familiar with its contents you will become.

To start annotating, click on the pen tool on the floating toolbar, so that the full toolbar appears. The colour and type of line (such as highlighter, paint brush and so on) can be changed with the Colour Palette, and the width of the pen with the Pen Width tool. While the annotation tools are active, the document being annotated is not active, and vice versa. For example, if the annotation tools are used to edit a passage in Word, Word itself will be inactive and changes cannot be made to the passage in Word. To stop annotating so that the other document can be edited, click the PC icon on the floating toolbar. This will make the annotation layer disappear, and the other document will become active again.

Tools>Colour Palette

Tools>Pen Width

Annotations over another application can be saved as a flipchart page. To ensure this happens click on Settings>Option Settings>General and select the Write directly on Desktop option (this should be set as the default). Then do the annotation required. Alternatively, annotations can be pasted into the original document if it is in Word, PowerPoint or Excel. To do this, select the 'Capture Desktop and Write on it' option in Settings>Option>Settings>General. This captures an image of the screen with the annotations on a new flipchart page, which can be pasted back to the original document by clicking on Edit>Paste in MS-Office document. The annotation is then an object in Word rather than live text.

Clicking once on an object (image or text) will select it. It will have resizing handles and can be dragged around the page. Double-clicking on text opens up an editing box. Either single- or double-clicking also provides a Menu, which has options for editing the object. These options can also be accessed from icons on the floating toolbar, or through the StarBoard menus. The bottom option on the Menu, Object Property, allows different font type, formatting and colour to be selected for text, or the colour and line width of an object drawn with the pen to be changed. Figure 6.13 shows the Object Property dialogue boxes for text and for shapes – these do not appear simultaneously and are just shown together here for illustration.

Objects and text can be grouped, aligned or distributed using the Edit menu. The Edit menu also contains:

- Cut
- Copy
- Paste
- Delete
- Clear

You will probably find you use these frequently, and that they are well worth putting onto the floating toolbar.

Edit>Cut

Edit>Copy

Edit>Paste

Edit>Delete

Edit>Clear

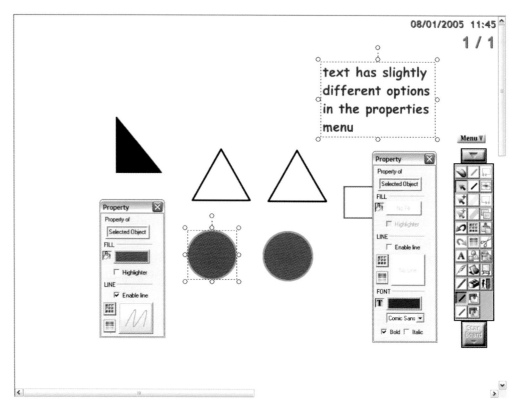

Figure 6.13 Editing text and objects

Writing and drawing freehand

To write or draw freehand, select the pen icon on the floating toolbar, then choose the pen type, colour and line width you want from the Colour Palette and Pen Width tool, and start writing or drawing. Objects such as rectangles and circles can be drawn using Tools>Objects.

To remove freehand writing or drawing, actions can be undone one at a time with the Undo tool and can be replaced with the Redo tool. Alternatively, there is an Eraser tool on the floating toolbar and Clear and Delete options in the Edit menu. The eraser can be used to remove part of an annotation, leaving the rest still joined as a single object. The Clear option removes all objects from a page. To use the Delete option, select the object to be deleted first.

Tools>Intelli-pen

The Intelli-pen is extremely useful for converting freehand lines and shapes into something recognisable. Start by clicking on the Intelli-pen icon on the floating toolbar or access it from the Tools menu. Then try drawing a square, circle or arrow – these should be converted to regular shapes as shown in Figure 6.14. Shapes can be filled with colour by editing them (as in Figure 6.13).

Note that the original drawing and the converted shape do not actually appear together – they are both shown here for illustration, but in reality the converted shape takes the place of the original drawing. Use the Undo and Redo icons to

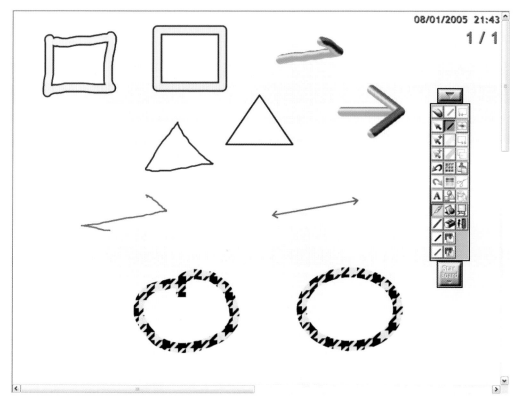

Figure 6.14 The StarBoard Intelli-pen

toggle between the original drawing and the converted shape. If the Grid is activated, whether it is showing or not, shapes created by the Intelli-pen will be snapped to the grid.

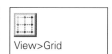

View>Grid

To convert handwriting to text, select the Handwriting tool and then just start writing. This tool recognises both letters and numbers. Handwriting recognition only works with the board attached, however, whereas shape recognition works whether the board is attached or not.

Settings>FEP>On

Inserting typed text

To insert typed text, click on the Text tool and then draw out a text box. The size of this text box will determine the font size. If the font size is too big or too small, select the text and use the resizing handles. This will change the font size, but not the layout of the text. The ENTER key should be used to spread text over more than one line. Alternatively, to get the formatting that you want you could type text in Word and then copy and paste into a text box.

Tools>Objects>Text

You can choose options for font type and colour by clicking on the text so that the Menu appears, then selecting Object Properties. Text can be removed by selecting it, then deleting it, or by using the Clear icon on the floating toolbar. To edit text, double click on it, and the text box will reappear to allow editing. The on-screen keyboard can be accessed through Mode>Accessories; it will appear accompanied by a text box. Editing and font choice is the same as for text typed from the ordinary keyboard.

Inserting images

Figure 6.15 shows a new page created with a background, images, typed text, handwritten text and straight lines produced with the Intelli-pen. On the far right is the floating toolbar. The map and swastika flags are taken from the clipart avail-

Tools>Clip-Art

View>Cover/
Uncover Sheet

able in the StarBoard software. The map has been resized to fit the page and then made part of the background by clicking on Edit>Stack Order>To Base Sheet. This has the advantage that the map no longer responds to the pen, so that it can be annotated, and annotations moved around without moving the map. Use Cover/Uncover Sheet to edit the map after it has been put into the background. This will hide any objects on the upper layer and make the map live again. Clicking on Cover/Uncover Sheet again will put the map back onto the background and show any objects on the upper layer.

A wealth of resources can be accessed from the clipart folders, which can be used as discrete objects or set as backgrounds, as above. To use an item from the clipart folders, just drag it onto the page. To remove it, select it and then click on the Delete icon on the floating toolbar. Objects can be resized by selecting them,

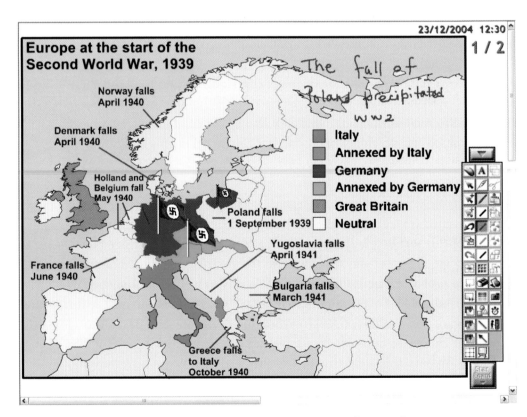

Figure 6.15 Creating a typical StarBoard page (WWII.yar)

then dragging on the resizing handles, or rotated using the rotation handle at the top of the object. Clicking on an object also opens the Menu, giving options to edit the object, alter which layer it is on, align it with other objects or group it with other objects.

Backgrounds

The Template icon opens up folders with a wide range of backgrounds, including lined paper, graph paper, maps, number squares, sports pitches, buildings, and many others. Backgrounds can be edited by removing them from the base layer using Cover/Uncover Sheet. A grid can be used either on a blank page or superimposed on a background. To activate the grid, click the Grid icon and then choose either Show Grid Line or Activate Grid or both. Activate Grid means that lines will snap to the grid. The grid size can be changed through Option Settings>Adjustment.

Documents>
Templates

View>Grid

You can also make your own backgrounds to save and use in future flipcharts. Click on Page List and then select the page. Then click on Save>Export selected page as an image. Save the page to the Template folder, which is likely to be in C:\Program Files\Hitachi Software Engineering\StarBoard software\Image\ Background.

Special tools

The StarBoard software includes Verdict, which is a voting system for multiple-choice questions. Many IWBs offer similar voting systems, but these are not normally available in the standard software. Voting systems are designed to help teachers keep track of who selects each option, so that individual progress can be monitored as well as checking how well the whole class understands a topic. It is also possible to make voting anonymous, so that it can be used with more sensitive questions.

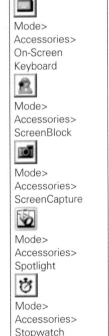

Mode>
Accessories>
On-Screen
Keyboard

Mode>
Accessories>
ScreenBlock

Mode>
Accessories>
ScreenCapture

Mode>
Accessories>
Spotlight

Mode>
Accessories>
Stopwatch

Mode>Accessories contains several special tools:

⊙ On-screen Keyboard

⊙ ScreenBlock

⊙ ScreenCapture

⊙ Spotlight

⊙ Stopwatch

The ScreenBlock puts a screen across any page in a flipchart or other application, which can then be moved down or sideways

Figure 6.16 Flipchart page showing ScreenBlock

from the right, so that material can be slowly revealed, as in Figure 6.16. Here a picture of Shakespeare has been superimposed on the screen. This is done by clicking on the screen, then selecting Open Image File. This particular image is to be found in the History>Tudor folder of the clipart. The original image is not the right file type to use directly, but if it is put on a page and an image of the page saved to a clipart folder, then it will be saved in the right format. The screen can be lowered to show one line of text at a time. To remove the screen, click on it and select Exit.

Capture Full
Capture Window
Capture Partial
Automatic Paste

It is possible to save individual images as well as whole pages in the clipart folders for future use. To do this, create the image, and then use the ScreenCapture tool to take a snapshot of the image. When the ScreenCapture options appear, click the small, square icon on the bottom right and set Save as file; Automatic Paste also puts a copy on the current flipchart page. Then select the third option, Capture Partial, which captures a specified area. Mark the area you want to capture. It will automatically be pasted onto the current flipchart page and a dialogue box to save it will be opened. Save it to a clipart folder (the filepath is likely to be C:\Program Files\Hitachi Software Engineering\StarBoard software\Image\ClipArt). This process saves an image of the object, rather than the object itself, so it will no longer be editable, other than by resizing and rotating. However, it is a useful way to save images and diagrams that you want to use frequently.

The other two options for the ScreenCapture tool are Capture Full, which captures the entire desktop (including toolbars), and Capture Window, which captures the selected window. Capture Full will paste the image to the background layer of a new flipchart page (if Automatic Paste is selected), while Capture Window will paste the image as an object onto a new page. Because images are initially captured to the clipboard and can be pasted into any application from there, this is an extremely useful tool. A picture can be taken of anything on the computer screen, including web images and pages, then pasted into Word, PowerPoint or a flipchart.

The Spotlight gives a movable spotlight, which can be used to light up and enlarge the spotlit part of the screen. It can be used over any application. The Stopwatch puts a clock over any application, which can be set to any time interval and can also play a sound when the time is up.

Other tools can be accessed through the clipart folders. In Maths>Angles there is a protractor which can be enlarged and rotated so that it can be used to measure angles on a flipchart page. Maths>Measure contains a ruler that is marked in a scale of five units to a division. Again, this can be enlarged and rotated so that it can be used to make real measurements. It can also be used as a blank scale. An alternative source of special mathematical tools is the selection from Mult-e-Maths which is provided with the StarBoard software: the Fraction Toolbox and the Shape and Space Toolbox.

The Fraction Toolbox (on the right in Figure 6.17) contains the:

◉ Text tool – allowing fractions to be correctly written

◉ Fraction wall

◉ Equivalence machine

◉ Multi-link cubes – to show fractions of quantities

◉ Fractions of circles

◉ Fractions of squares

The fractions of the circle or square can be rotated, reflected and translated so they are useful for a variety of topics in addition to fractions.

The Shape and Space Toolbox (left in Figure 6.17) contains many two- and three-dimensional shapes. There are also angles with rotating lines, protractors and co-ordinate axes which can have points put on them, either ready labelled or blank for students to label. Different faces on a three-dimensional shape can be coloured differently so that when the shape is rotated it is possible to see what happens to individual faces from different perspectives, as in Figure 6.18.

Here, the three smaller pyramid images were produced separately, then the whole put together in image-editing software to produce this picture. In reality, only one image of a particular shape will appear at a time. Inset on the top left of

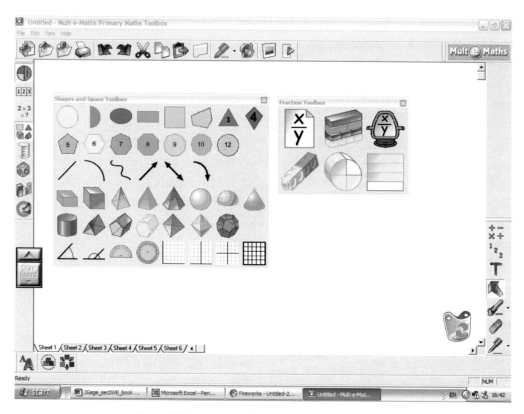

Figure 6.17 Fraction and Shape and Space Toolboxes

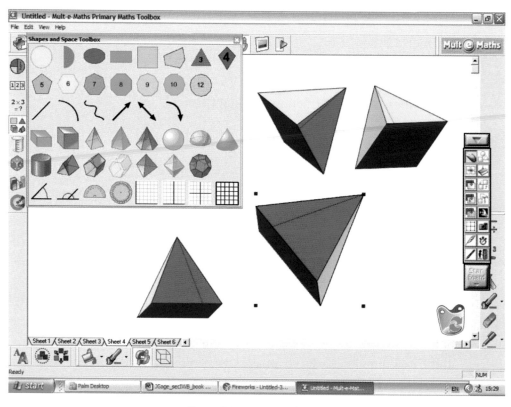

Figure 6.18 Creating shapes

Figure 6.18 is the Shape and Space Toolbox, showing the choice of shapes available. On the bottom left is the Shape and Space toolbar, which shows the options available for a shape.

Incorporating sounds, video, other files and hyperlinks

To make a hyperlink to a website, simply type the full URL (including the http:// at the beginning) into a text box on a flipchart page. If the computer has an internet connection, this will then link directly to the site.

Files of all types, including sound and video, can be opened from a flipchart so that they are quickly available during a lesson. To do this, the file needs to be saved in the Favourites folder, and in order to facilitate finding linked files during a lesson it would certainly be worth putting the Favourites icon on the floating toolbar. As more files are put into this

Documents>
Favourites>Add
Favourite

folder it would also be a good idea to sort them into sub-folders to make it easier to find them. To open a file, click on Favourites to open the folder, then click on the blue arrow at the left of the required file. This gives the option to open, rename or delete that file. Opening a file other than Word, PowerPoint or Excel is then straightforward.

If you open an MS Office document in this way, however, you are likely to find that the pages are imported into a flipchart, rather than opened in the original Office application. If you want the original document to open, it is necessary first to change some of the Settings. Click on Settings>Option Setting. In the dialogue box that appears, first select the General tab. The first two options are 'Capture Desktop and Write on it' and 'Write Directly on Desktop'. Capture Desktop and Write on it is the default mode, in which Office files are captured as a flipchart page, which can then be annotated in the flipchart. To open the original file, select instead Write Directly on Desktop. This option allows you to annotate directly on the desktop and then to save your annotations in the original Office file.

Open the Documents tab on the Option Settings dialogue box again. When Capture Desktop and Write on it is selected, the options for PowerPoint, Word and Excel are greyed out. When Write Directly on Desktop is selected there will be options to Browse, Edit or Allow User to Select. Browse does the same as Capture Desktop and Write on it, importing the pages of the file into a flipchart. Edit allows the original file to be opened. This file can be used both in the original application and annotated with the StarBoard tools. Both types of change can be saved; to save annotations into the original file, use the Paste in MS Office Document icon. Allow User to Select means that a dialogue box will

Edit>Paste in
MS-Office
Document

appear when the user tries to open a document giving the choice of Browse and Edit modes.

This brief overview of the StarBoard software is not exhaustive, but there should be plenty here to get you started. To find out more, there are useful guides available on the Cambridge-Hitachi website (see Appendix 1).

PowerPoint or IWB software?

Presentations can be created in both PowerPoint and IWB software. If you only have a data projector, then you have no choice about which to use. However, if you have an IWB, you may wonder which is better. It really depends on how you wish to use your presentation and what content you wish to incorporate. Depending on the IWB software you have, however, you may find you have a greater range of resources such as page templates or backgrounds in the IWB software. Moving objects or rotating them during a presentation is easy to do in IWB software. This could be done in PowerPoint through animation but would be very time-consuming to prepare; IWB software allows a much more dynamic presentation which does not need all animations and movement to be prepared in advance. The effects are also considerably more convincing, particularly for smooth rotations.

It is possible to do nearly everything you can do in PowerPoint in IWB software, and vice versa. Some things are more easily achieved in one type of software than the other, but this will depend on what type of IWB software you have. Experimentation will be necessary to explore what your IWB software will do, and whether it is easier to achieve a given effect with that or with PowerPoint.

CHAPTER 7

Teaching strategies

In this chapter, various techniques useful for producing lesson materials or using them in the classroom are described. These are illustrated with the resources available on the accompanying CD. File names of resources are given in the picture captions, and other files that demonstrate the same technique are given at the end of each section. (Note: where a file extension is not shown in a picture caption, it is available in SMARTBoard .xbk format, AS2 .flp format and StarBoard .yar format.)

Resources are not categorised here by curriculum area as most of the techniques discussed can be used in many different curriculum areas. To use the resources, decide what effect you wish to achieve, then see if there is a resource that contains that effect. The content can then be edited to suit the lesson you wish to offer. Some of the resources are in the form of templates that can be adapted to many different lessons. The CD also contains notes and full details of content and techniques used in individual files in *Notes_on_resources.doc*.

Annotating over an existing document

One of the simplest ways to start using an IWB is to use an existing document, perhaps reformatted for whole-class use, and to use the IWB tools to annotate it. The annotations can then be saved separately or with the document for future use or to print out. This technique is particularly useful for lessons where original text is to be analysed, as illustrated in Figure 4.1 (p.37) and Figure 6.16 (p.86). The class can all be focused on the same page at the same time, helping to maintain concentration and pace.

Annotating a document can be used for many purposes besides analysing text, from demonstrating how software is to be used to modelling how to do a particular activity or going through the intricacies of a calculation. For example, Figure 7.1 shows an Excel spreadsheet annotated to generate discussion

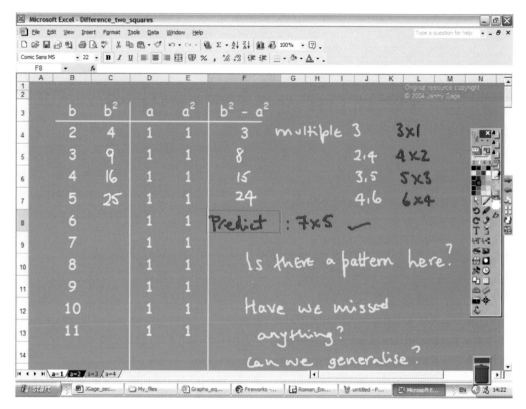

Figure 7.1 Use of annotation tools on a spreadsheet (Difference_two_squares.xls)

about whether there is a pattern in the answers found which might lead to a generalisation.

CD: all files are suitable for annotation

Using images

There are very few presentations that cannot be made more interesting and informative by the addition of images of some kind. These do not need to be complicated or difficult to produce. Digital photos, clipart, diagrams or images scanned into the computer from a textbook or the web can be very effective, as can simple diagrams created using the Draw toolbar in MS Office applications or Paint (see Chapter 5).

La_Casa.ppt (Figure 7.2) uses text, digital photos and computer-produced diagrams on PowerPoint slides to stimulate oral discussion, in this case in an MFL resource. This technique could be used in many other curriculum areas, however, where the objective is to prompt discussion. It is very straightforward to create diagrams like this in MS Office applications or Paint, or diagrams can be hand-drawn and scanned into the computer. The advantage of using such presentations in a lesson is that they can be tailored specifically to fit the lesson objectives and needs of the students in a way that no commercially produced presentation or textbook picture can.

Figure 7.2 PowerPoint presentation with text, photos and diagram (La_Casa.ppt)

There is a huge variety of images available in the clipart included with MS Office and with IWB software, which can be used to illustrate presentations or to create quick resources in many curriculum areas. Figure 7.3 shows four single-page resources made from clipart pictures available within the software shown. Making resources like these takes very little time, but provides an interesting visual starting point for discussion.

In *Roman Emperors.ppt* (Figure 7.4), an image of Tiberius has been scanned and pasted onto the first page together with his obituary. An obituary like this can be created in Paint by scanning a real newspaper obituary into the computer to use as a background, then putting text boxes with a transparent background (lowest icon on the left-hand toolbar in Paint) over it. This provides not only an opportunity to discuss the reign of various Roman emperors, but also what an obituary of them might say.

We can also take the text and work on it collectively. Most scanners include optical character recognition software (OCR) such as Textbridge. This will read the words on the scanned page and turn them into a text document. Sometimes you will need to edit this, but such programs are becoming increasingly accurate.

In Figure 7.5 the same text has been scanned into MSWord so that everyone can discuss what the key achievements of Tiberius's rule were.

We can pick out key elements of the text in a number of ways. One is to use the Highlight tool to pick them out on the screen (Figure 7.6).

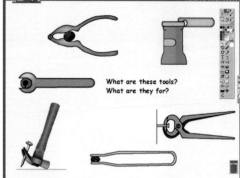

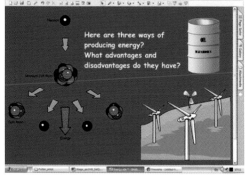

Figure 7.3 Using clipart (Das_Wetter, Tools, Religions, Energy)

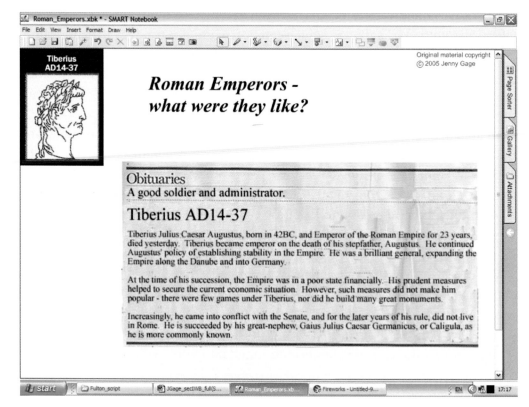

Figure 7.4 Creating images in Paint (Roman_Emperors)

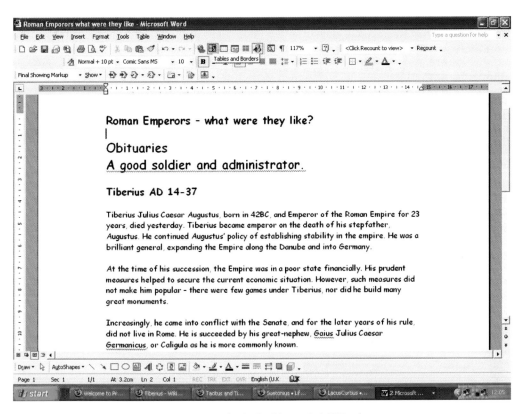

Figure 7.5 Tiberius's obituary in MSWord

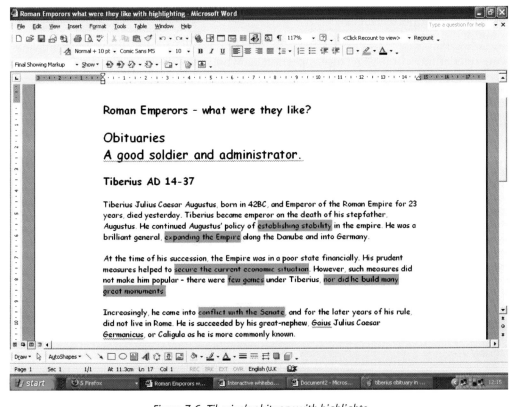

Figure 7.6 Tiberius's obituary with highlights

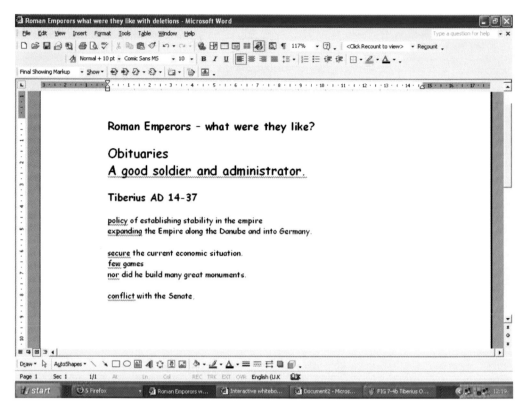

Figure 7.7 Tiberius's obituary with irrelevant text deleted

Or we could simply delete the other text and just be left with the key points of his time as Emperor (Figure 7.7).

Texts can be easily copied from the internet simply by highlighting the words you need then choosing copy, opening a MSWord document and pasting. You should note the source so that issues of copyright can be addressed.

CD: Since many of the resources contain images, this list only contains those not illustrated in this book:

Finding_formulae.flp

Finding_formulae.ppt

Finding_formulae.xbk

Finding_formulae.yar

Hot_cold_cubes.ppt

Today.flp

Today.ppt

Today.xbk

Today.yar

Tree_diagrams.ppt

Displaying students' work

Students can create their own presentations in PowerPoint or in IWB software for display on the IWB to the whole class, for discussion, redrafting or simply to celebrate student achievement. Work done on paper or in books can also be scanned into the computer for display or to add to a portfolio for assessment purposes. Figure 7.8 shows PowerPoint slides created from students' original writing, drawings and clipart. These presentations also contain sound files of the students speaking their text aloud.

Figure 7.8 Displaying students' work: Student2-French.ppt, Student1-French.ppt, Student-Spanish.ppt, Student2-French.ppt

CD: Student1_French.ppt, Student2_French.ppt, Student_Spanish.ppt

Copying and pasting from one page to another

Another straightforward use of IWB software is to facilitate copying and pasting content from one page to another. The page could be in an IWB flipchart/notebook or it might be a PowerPoint slide, a Word page, or from any other application. Where the pages are in IWB software, copy-and-paste techniques for that particular software can be used, although it may be easier to use the IWB Screen Capture or Camera tool to copy part or all of a page to paste it into another page or application.

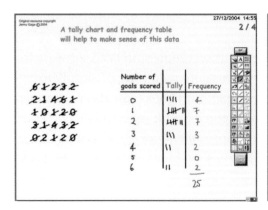
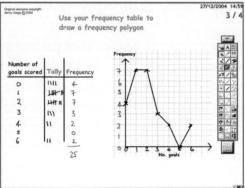

Figure 7.9 Using copy-and-paste from one flipchart/notebook page to another (Handling_data)

In Figure 7.9, a tally chart and frequency table completed on one page have been copied and pasted onto the next page so that the information can be used to plot a frequency polygon.

CD: Handling_data.flp, Handling_data.ppt, Handling_data.xbk, Handling_data.yar, Population_statistics.flp, Population_statistics.ppt, Population_statistics.xbk, Population_statistics.yar

Links to the internet or other documents

If a particular lesson requires a number of documents or web pages, these can all be linked through a flipchart/notebook or PowerPoint presentation. The advantage of doing this is that the whole lesson is then contained within one document, so that switching between resources is made quick and easy. A resource where this technique has been used is *Pythagoras*, in which students are helped to create a proof of Pythagoras's Theorem. A link to a dynamic geometry file (in Geometers' Sketchpad) can then be used to demonstrate the proof.

Figure 7.10 shows a notebook/flipchart page, with the proof added using the IWB annotation tools. The attached Geometers' Sketchpad (GS) file is open in a separate window to the left of the IWB page. Depending on the type of IWB software you have, it may be possible to show both files simultaneously. If not, it is very easy to move rapidly from one to the other.

Dragging on the point marked B on the GS diagram allows the diagram to be moved about and resized. The figures displayed will then show how the lengths change as the diagram is moved about, demonstrating that Pythagoras's Theorem always remains true. Putting the algebraic proof alongside a geometrical demonstration can be used to help students see that demonstration is not proof, but that it can be used to illuminate proof.

CD: Coins_Investigation.flp, Coins_Investigation.ppt, Coins_Investigation. xbk, Coins_Investigation.xls, Coins_Investigation.yar,

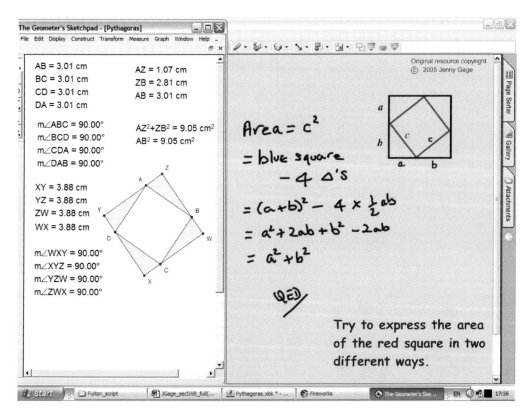

Figure 7.10 IWB notebook/flipchart with linked file (Pythagoras)

Difference_two_squares.flp, Difference_two_squares.ppt,
Difference_two_squares.xbk, Difference_two_squares. xls,
Difference_two_squares.yar, Investigating_Fibonacci_numbers.flp,
Investigating_Fibonacci_numbers.ppt, Investigating_Fibonacci_numbers.xbk,
Investigating_Fibonacci_numbers.xls, Investigating_Fibonacci_numbers.yar,
Pythagoras.flp, Pythagoras.gsp, Pythagoras.ppt,
Pythagoras.xbk, Pythagoras.yar

Revealing information gradually and giving feedback

Hide and reveal techniques

The screen available in IWB software can be used to reveal the contents of a page,
bit by bit, as shown in Figure 6.16 (p.86). Most IWB screens can be used with any
application, not just over flipcharts/notebooks.

Worksheets containing diagrams without labels or with a problem to solve can
be printed out from an IWB page or other application. However, the page on the
IWB could already have labels and/or answers on it, all ready to be revealed on-
screen once students have had a chance to think about them. The IWB annotation
tools can be used to add a layer the same colour as the background colour of a page,

concealing text or other objects, which is then erased or removed to reveal what is underneath, as in the images in Figure 7.11.

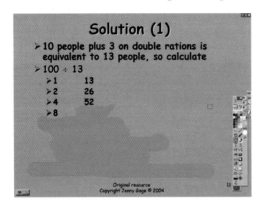

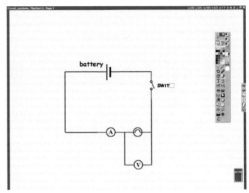

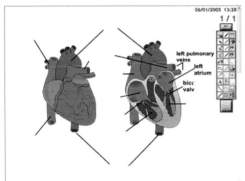

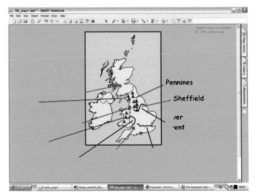

Figure 7.11 Using the IWB annotation tools to hide and reveal information
(Egyptian_fractions.ppt, Circuit_symbols, Heart, UK_map1)

Select text
Edit>Select all
Ctrl A
Font colour

A ▾

Format>Font
(Word)
or
Format>Cells
(Excel)
Ctrl 1
Undo

↺

Edit>Undo
Ctrl Z

Another technique similar to this is to use a font colour that is the same colour as the background colour in Word or Excel. When students have had a chance to consider what a label or answer should be, the font colour can be changed to reveal the answer. This is shown in Figure 7.12, where missing words can be added with the annotation tools in the spaces in a text. The choice of green for the background colour is deliberate, emphasising the green gas clouds.

Changing the font colour of the missing words then shows whether the correct choices were made. To change the font colour quickly in either Word or Excel, select all the text, then choose a font colour which shows up against the background. Then Undo the font colour change to put the document back to its original state for re-use.

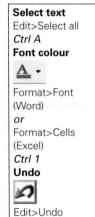

CD: Arithmetic_practice.xls, Circuit_symbols.flp,
Circuit_symbols.xbk, Circuit_symbols.yar, Difference_two_squares.flp,
Difference_two_squares.xbk, Difference_two_squares.yar, Directed_number.xls,
Heart.flp, Heart.xbk, Heart.yar, Pythagoras.flp, Pythagoras.xbk, Pythagoras.yar,
Think_of_a_number.flp, Think_of_a_number.xbk, Think_of_a_number.yar,
UK_map1.flp, UK_map1.xbk, UK_map1.yar, W_Owen.doc

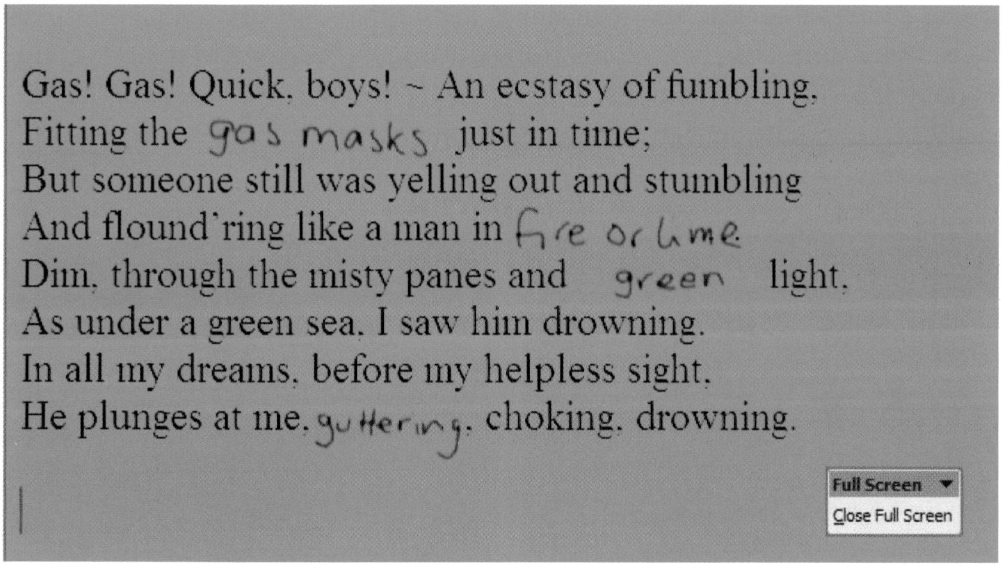

Gas! Gas! Quick, boys! ~ An ecstasy of fumbling,
Fitting the gas masks just in time;
But someone still was yelling out and stumbling
And flound'ring like a man in fire or lime
Dim, through the misty panes and green light,
As under a green sea, I saw him drowning.
In all my dreams, before my helpless sight,
He plunges at me, guttering, choking, drowning.
Full Screen
Close Full Screen

Figure 7.12 Using colour to conceal text (W_Owen.doc)

Using dynamic techniques to reveal information

Dynamic techniques, such as PowerPoint animations or dragging away covering shapes in IWB software, can be used to reveal information. In Figure 7.13, the left-hand image shows a flipchart/notebook where the answer is already on the page but hidden from view by a shape that has to be moved aside. The right-hand image shows the same resource, this time using a PowerPoint animation, which displays the answer only when the mouse is clicked, causing the answer of '10' to fly onto the page.

PowerPoint can be used to make simple animations to bring presentations to life or to reveal information gradually. In *Theories of the Universe.ppt*, information is presented, bit by bit, allowing discussion of individual issues and diagrams. In Figure 7.14, the left-hand image shows a slide with diagram and title. A second click of the mouse gives the slide shown in the right-hand image, in which the diagram is slightly reduced in size and moved to the right so that important points

Think of a number ...
Write down any integer
Multiply it by 2
Add 6
Divide by 2
Subtract the number you first thought of
What do you get?
The answer is always 3.
Move the shape to see the answer.
Think of a number ...
Write down any integer
Add 5
Multiply by 2
Subtract twice the number you started with
What do you get?
You always get
10
Original resource copyright Jenny Gage © 2004

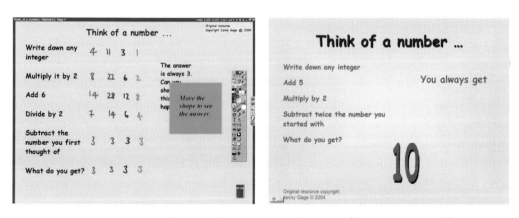

Figure 7.13 Using dynamic techniques to reveal answers (Think_of_a_number)

can be summarised next to it. The appearance of the summary can be controlled by you so that the class has an opportunity to discuss the diagram first, observing important points for themselves. The diagram shown here was created using specialist drawing software, but could equally be an image scanned in from the web or a book.

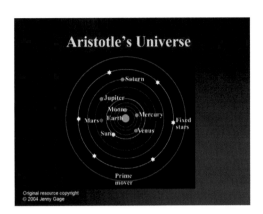 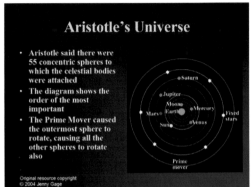

Figure 7.14 Animations in PowerPoint

Trouble-shooting animations can be more time-consuming than simply putting text or images onto a slide, but is well worth trying from time to time to create more impact or to help make a difficult concept clearer. This is demonstrated in *Hot_cold_cubes.ppt*, in which red and blue cubes are animated to demonstrate what happens when positive and negative numbers are added and subtracted.

 CD: Angle_estimation.xls, Difference_two_squares.ppt,
Egyptian_arithmetic.ppt, Graphs_equations.ppt, Hot_cold_cubes.ppt,
Pythagoras.ppt, Theories_Universe.ppt, Think_of_a_number.flp,
Think_of_a_number.ppt, Think_of_a_number.xbk,
Think_of_a_number.yar, Tree_diagrams.ppt

Using hyperlinks for multiple choice questions and answers

Yet another way to reveal answers gradually is to use hyperlinks in PowerPoint. Text can be linked to another page where the answer to a question is given, or the instruction to try again. In Figure 7.15, the images show a sequence of slides.

In the first slide, students are invited to choose parts of speech from a list. The wrong option ('but') is chosen for an article. Clicking on the word 'but' displays a slide saying 'Try again!'. Clicking this text links back to the original slide, so that another choice can be made. The original choice is now shown in a different colour, so students can see what they chose previously. The final slide shows what happens when the correct choice of 'the' is made. This is linked to the next slide with a new choice to be made. This strategy of linking PowerPoint slides with hyperlinks can be adapted for all kinds of multiple-choice resources. It can also be used in AS2, where objects can be linked to other pages in a flipchart.

Figure 7.15 *Using hyperlinks to reveal whether an answer is correct or not (Parts_of_speech.ppt)*

CD: Parts_of_speech.flp, Parts_of_speech.ppt

Using an 'IF' formula to give feedback in Excel

Feedback can be given in Excel by the use of an 'IF' formula. The formula *=IF(condition,'insert text for correct answer', 'insert text for incorrect answer')* can be used to tell students if the answer they have given is correct or not. In Figure 7.16, the left-hand image shows fractions that are not equivalent to the ratio above them, and the right-hand image shows the corrected figures.

The formula used in this case is *=IF(S8=T8,(IF(S9=T9,"well done!","try again")), "try again")*. This contains an 'IF' formula nested within another 'IF' formula – if the first fraction and ratio are equivalent, then the formula goes on to look at the second pair. If both are correct, 'well done!' appears, as in the right-hand image. If either pair is incorrect, 'try again!' results, as in the left-hand image. Cells S8, T8, S9 and T9 contain the four fractions/ratios expressed as decimals and are used to calculate the fractions and ratios from the cells in the B and D columns where numbers can be inserted by students. All the formulae used in this and other Excel resources can be found from the files on the accompanying CD.

CD: Fractions_decimals_ratio.xls

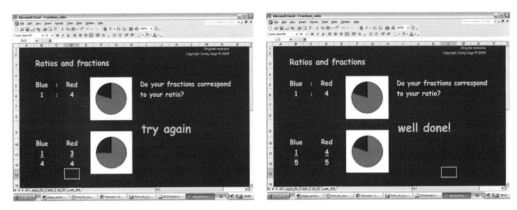

Figure 7.16 An 'IF' formula used in Excel to provide answers (Fractions_decimals_ratio.xls)

Dynamic techniques

Various techniques which can be used with an IWB make direct use of the dynamic possibilities afforded by PowerPoint and IWB software. PowerPoint animations can be used to produce dynamic effects and these are covered in the section on providing feedback. Other dynamic techniques include moving objects to sort, match or compare them, and using the rotation and reflection properties of IWB software.

Sorting, matching and comparing

This technique can be used in a great variety of resources using IWB flipcharts/notebooks, some of which are shown in Figure 7.17.

In the top-left image in Figure 7.17, questions to answer are shown in blue, and these need to be matched to sources of information shown in yellow. Both are made from text boxes with coloured backgrounds. If text boxes cannot be given a coloured background in a particular IWB software, a coloured rectangle of the appropriate size can be put behind the text box and the two grouped together so that they move as a single object. In the top-right image, circles produced with the annotation tools are dragged onto a diagram to help students see how to find the perimeter of a shape. In the bottom-left image, parts of the verb in French need to be put together then matched with their English equivalents. In the bottom-right image, labels for a diagram need to be dragged to the right place on the diagram.

Figure 7.18 demonstrates a way of making comparisons that are particularly useful with Excel. The IWB annotation tools are used to give answers to the questions in the spreadsheet (left-hand image), then a snapshot is taken with the ScreenCapture tool. This can be immediately pasted back into Excel, so that the answers given by students can be compared with those produced by Excel (right-hand image). The correct answers are revealed by changing the font colour. This resource also has an image of a number line copied from clipart available in IWB

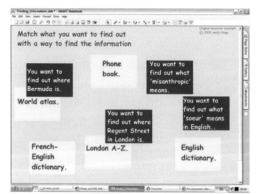

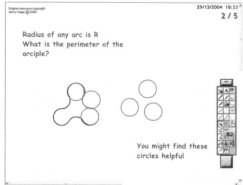

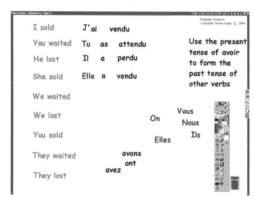

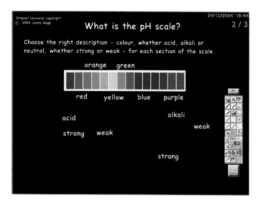

Figure 7.17 Sorting, matching and comparing (Finding_information, Arciple, Past_tense, Acids_alkalis)

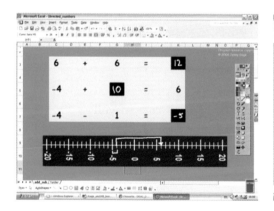

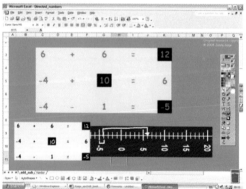

Figure 7.18 Using the screen capture annotation tool to compare answers in Excel
(Directed_Numbers.xls)

software and pasted into the spreadsheet to help students. Annotation tools have been used to show the results of the calculations on the number line.

CD: Acids_alkalis.flp, Acids_alkalis.xbk, Acids_alkalis.yar,
Arciple.flp, Arciple.ppt, Arciple.xbk, Arciple.yar, Arithmetic_practice.xls,
Directed_numbers.xls, Finding_information.flp, Finding_information.xbk,
Finding_information.yar, Graphs_equations.flp, Graphs_equations.xbk,
Graphs_equations.yar, Matching_expressions.flp, Matching_ expressions.xbk,
Matching_expressions.yar, Past_tense.flp, Past_tense.xbk, Past_tense. yar,
UK_map2.flp, UK_map2.xbk, UK_map2.yar

Rotating and reflecting images

Rotation and reflection of images is particularly useful in maths resources: mathematical techniques which are impossible to demonstrate on an ordinary whiteboard can easily be shown on an IWB. Shapes can be rotated in most IWB

XY-origin

Rotate

Rotate
automatically

software, although it may not be possible to change the point about which rotation occurs. AS2 and the StarBoard Shape and Space Toolbox both allow the centre of rotation to be moved, but the SMARTBoard does not. In AS2 there is an icon for XY-origin in the Presentation Toolset, which can be dragged onto the floating toolbar. Positioning this icon sets both the centre of rotation and the line about which reflections occur. On the StarBoard, if an object from the Shape and Space Toolbox is selected, options will appear on the bottom toolbar that include two rotation options. Either of these allows the centre of rotation to be moved.

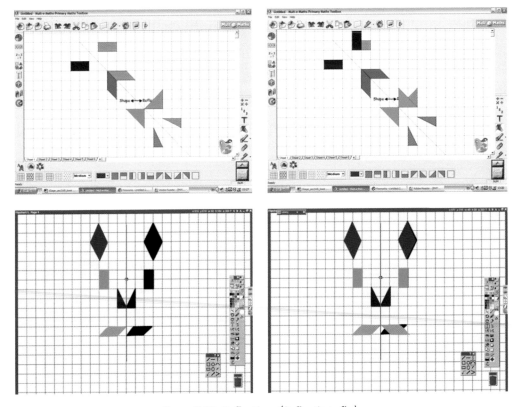

Figure 7.19 Reflections (Reflections.flp)

Objects can be reflected in AS2 and with the StarBoard Shape and Space Toolbox, but not on the SMARTBoard. The two left-hand images in Figure 7.19 show shapes with a reflection line and reflected (monochromatic) shapes that have been added by hand (using the Shape Recognition tool in AS2 and the polygon tool from the Shape and Space Toolbox on the StarBoard). The two right-hand images show reflected shapes added by the IWB software, giving students feedback on their suggestions.

Reflections can be done about either a horizontal or vertical axis in AS2, using the XY-origin tool to set the mirror line. Once the line is set, select the object to be reflected, then right-click, and choose M>Edit>Flip or Reflect>X or Y axis. Flip reflects the original object, whereas Reflect leaves the original object in place and reflects a copy of it. In the StarBoard Shape and Space Toolbox, reflection lines can be added from the bottom toolbar, and these include lines at 45 degrees as well as horizontal and vertical lines. For more advanced work on rotations and reflections, dynamic geometry software, such as Geometers' Sketchpad or Cabri, provides more functionality.

CD: Reflections.flp

Designing simple games

Many games are available on the internet for use in a lesson via the IWB. The IWB can also be used to make simple games, such as the *Factor Game*, shown in Figure 7.20.

In this game the class and the teacher take it in turns to drag a number from its place on the left of the board, according to the Rules given at the top of the page. Creating a notebook/flipchart page for a game like this need only take a few minutes, but the game is then available as often as required. A simple game like this involves knowing about factors and multiples, prime numbers, and thinking

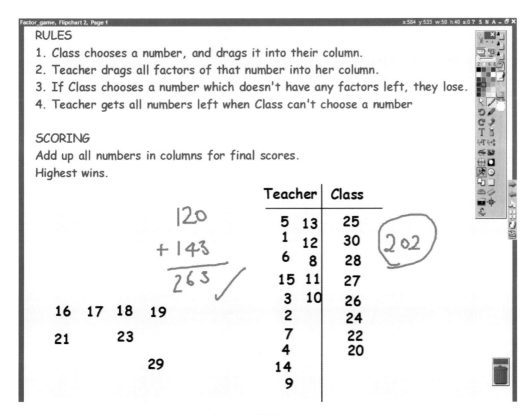

Figure 7.20 Factor game

up a good game strategy, so the educational return is well worth the investment in time in setting it up. Other simple games can be prepared equally quickly.

CD: Factor_game.flp, Factor_game.ppt, Factor_game.xbk,
Factor_game.yar, Squares.flp, Squares.ppt, Squares.xbk, Squares.yar

Using graphs

Basic graphing

Excel can be used to create many different types of graphs, although specialist graphing software, such as Autograph or Omnigraph, provides greater functionality. Alternatively, templates are available on the CD in IWB software so that graphs can be drawn by hand (see Figure 6.6, p.66).

In Figure 7.21, the top-left image shows axes available in the StarBoard Shapes and Space Toolbox; similar axes are available in most IWB software. A perfect straight-line graph can be drawn onto the axes with the straight-line annotation tool, showing immediately that one of the points has been calculated incorrectly. The top-right image shows graphs that have been copied from a graphing package and pasted onto an IWB page using the ScreenCapture tool. Formulae can then be dragged to match to each graph.

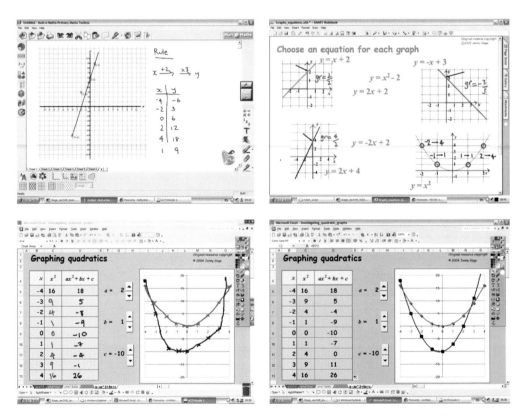

Figure 7.21 Graphs (Graphs_equations, Investigating_quadratic_graphs.xls)

The two bottom images show how Excel can be used to investigate graphs, since the coefficients in the equations can be changed using the 'sliders' provided in the resource. In the left-hand image, IWB annotation tools have been used to fill in a table of values and plot the resulting points. This is then contrasted with the graph obtained by using the formulae already on the spreadsheet that give the correct graph. The two can be compared with each other if the initial annotations are saved or copied and pasted back into the spreadsheet, enabling mistakes to be seen and discussed. Students also see perfect graphs, as well as hand-drawn attempts.

CD: Graphs_background.flp, Graphs_background.xbk,
Graphs_background.yar, Graphs_equations.flp, Graphs_equations.ppt,
Graphs_equations.xbk, Graphs_equations.yar,
Investigating_quadratic_graphs.xls, Straight_line_equations.xls

Illustrating data

Graphs can be used in a variety of curriculum areas to give visual emphasis to data. In Figure 7.22 graphs have been copied and pasted from previous pages in an IWB presentation, showing the difference in the demographics for Afghanistan and the UK in 2000. This could be used as a mathematical exercise or as the focus for a discussion in geography. The red line shows the median age for the population of each

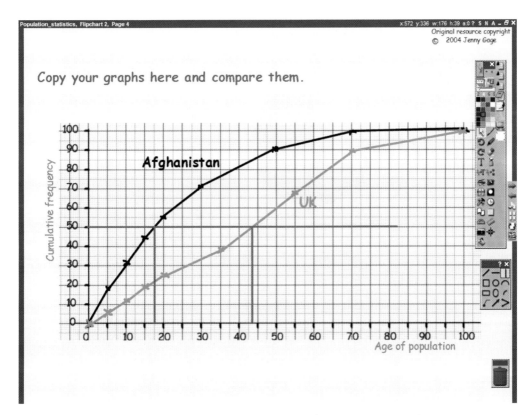

Figure 7.22 Illustrating data with graphs (Population_statistics)

country, showing very clearly that Afghanistan has a much younger population than the UK.

The CD also contains a template which can be used either to record the results of class votes or the responses to multiple-choice questions, or could be edited to show data for subsequent comment or interpretation.

CD: Graphs_template.xls, Handling_data.flp, Handling_data.ppt, Handling_data.xbk, Handling_data.yar, Interpreting_graphs.xls, Population_statistics.flp, Population_statistics.ppt, Population_statistics.xbk, Population_statistics.yar

Illustrating numbers

Excel graphs can be used to compare numbers, particularly for angles (Figure 7.23) and fractions, decimals and ratios (Figure 7.16, p.104).

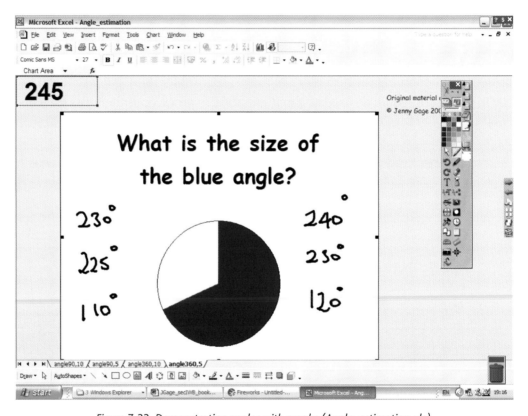

Figure 7.23 Demonstrating angles with graphs (Angle_estimation.xls)

A pie-chart can be used with random numbers to produce random angles for students to estimate – pressing F9 on the keyboard gives a new angle. In Figure 7.23 a few estimates are written onto the graph with the IWB annotation tools. The graph is then dragged to one side, revealing the correct answer in the top-left corner of the spreadsheet.

CD: Angle_estimation.xls, Fractions_decimals_ratio.xls

Using random numbers

Several of the resources created in Excel for the CD use random numbers, so that a new set of questions is always instantly available. In any of these, pressing F9 on the keyboard (on- or off-screen) will immediately give a new set of numbers.

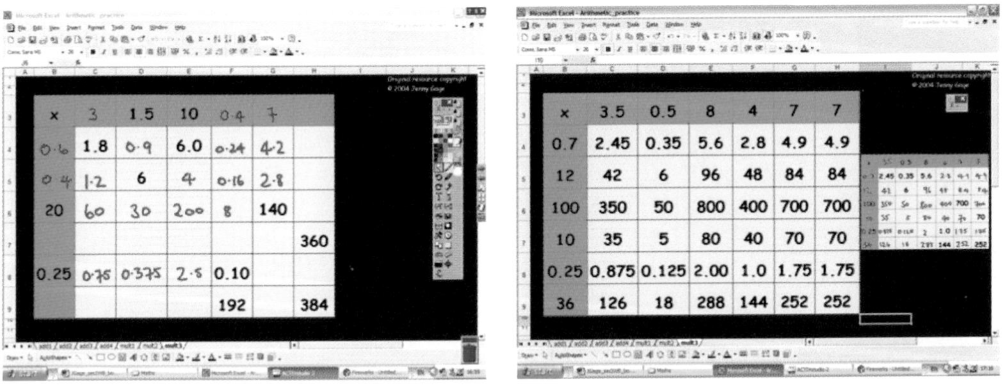

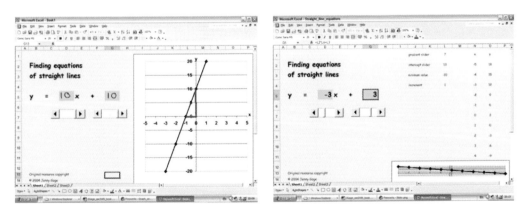

Figure 7.24 Using random numbers in Excel (Arithmetic_practice.xls)

Figure 7.24 shows an example of a spreadsheet based on numbers that are randomly chosen by Excel between certain limits. The left-hand image shows annotation over the spreadsheet, and the right-hand image shows how answers can be copied with the IWB ScreenCapture tool, then pasted back onto the spreadsheet for comparison with the correct answers. These can be revealed by changing the font colour of the spreadsheet, then changing it back for further use.

| **Select All** |
| Edit>Select All |
| *Ctrl A* |
| **Font colour** |
| **A** ▾ |
| Format>Cells>Font |
| *Ctrl 1*>Font |

Varying numbers can also be produced using a 'slider' as in Figure 7.25.

Figure 7.25 'Sliders' used in Excel to vary numbers (Straight_line_equations.xls)

Figure 7.25 shows horizontal sliders (these could just as easily be vertical sliders) which are set to generate integers hidden in cells D5 and G5. Students' suggestions for the gradient and intercept can be written onto the spreadsheet with the IWB annotation tools (left-hand image). Changing the font colour of these two cells will show what the gradient and intercept actually are, and therefore what the equation is (right-hand image). The values in D5 and G5 are set between −10 and 10, changing with an increment of 1. All these values can be altered by moving the graph aside to show the values used (right-hand image). Because a slider cannot be set with a minimum value or increment of less than zero, a simple formula, which can be seen and edited as required in the resource on the CD, has been used here to allow any minimum value and increment to be set.

CD: Angle_estimation.xls, Arithmetic_practice.xls, Directed_number.xls, Interpreting_graphs.xls, Investigating_quadratic_graphs.xls, Straight_line_equation.xls

CHAPTER 8

Additional software

What to look for in whiteboard software

When deciding on what software to use on your interactive whiteboard there are a number of practical and pedagogical pointers to take into consideration. First of all you need to think about its appearance and ask questions such as 'Does it have an easy-to-use, uncluttered interface?' On-screen buttons and icons should be kept to a minimum to remove distractions, and everything provided should add to what you can do rather than leave you wondering what each one is for. Secondly, are the menus and toolbars easy to reach? Some software such as Inspiration (see below) allows you to move the toolbar to the bottom of the screen so everyone can reach it. And finally, can it be seen easily from everywhere in the classroom? If not, can font sizes be adjusted and icons enlarged? You need software that lets you get on with teaching rather than demands that you spend your time trying to make it useful.

Similarly, you will want to choose software that supports your teaching, that lets you choose how you want to work, rather than programs that will only work in the way that they want. You need to be in charge, rather than the resource you are using being in charge. Broadly speaking, you will be looking for 'open' software, that is programs whose usefulness is not determined by their content but by their functionality – what they do. This leaves you to decide what element of the lesson the software, and therefore the whiteboard, will support. Generally speaking, programs that work well are effective because they help to support understanding, and are good for whole-class or group teaching where pupils are sharing knowledge and constructing understanding collectively.

Some programs are written to be used on a whiteboard, such as the suites that come with them; others adapt very well. One example of the former is Easiteach from RM which is a quick and easy way of preparing lessons and also has a number of packs of additional resources for specific subjects. In the example below, a Year 8 science lesson is using the Equipment images from the Science folder in the Multimedia resources bank to decide what would be needed for an experiment to mix iron and sulphur.

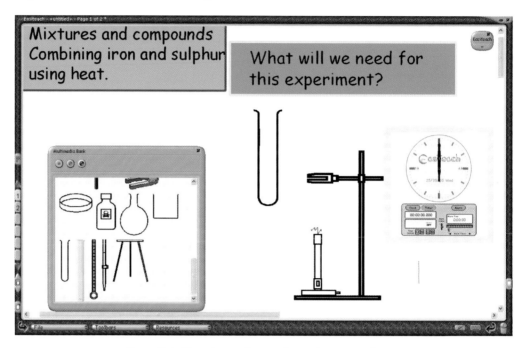

Figure 8.1 Choosing equipment for a science experiment

Before the lesson the teacher can put up the task title and a key question. On the board the Resources folder (found at the bottom of the screen for easy access) is open, as is the relevant section. Objects can then be simply dragged onto the screen, re-sized and grouped. A timer has been included from the 'Flash' folder as well, so pupils can record how long it takes for the iron sulphide to form.

Following the experiment, the diagram can be left on the board for pupils to copy. The teacher can annotate it using the handwriting recognition tool that then converts the words to text, or key words can be listed on the board and dragged into place.

Another page can then be opened up in Easiteach to explain what has happened (Figure 8.2).

Here pupils can come to the front and move atoms from one test tube to the other on the board, combining them to form molecules of iron sulphide. The word list is then used to complete the text box. The pupils can copy the diagram and text to their books, or it can be printed out for them all to have.

As well as the generic tools available with the basic software suite, Easiteach also has subject-specific resources that can be added on. The Maths set includes number squares, place value cards and a function machine, while the Literacy set has a cloze function and tools to structure writing. Easiteach Science set includes image capture to link to external devices such as a microscope, and web diagrams to show relationships between items and ideas.

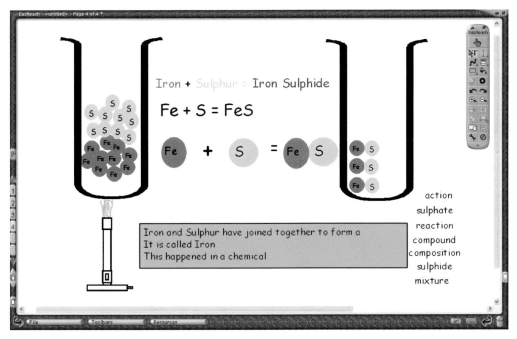

Figure 8.2 Outcome of the experiment

This last function is becoming quite common with the introduction of a number of mind-mapping programs. Here Inspiration has been used with the class to brainstorm about the work prior to writing up the experiment.

The process in Figure 8.3 is quite quick and individual elements of it can be re-coloured or given specific graphics to make the whole more memorable. Ideas can be added to the board, then links created afterwards. Some links have been given prompts to show the relationship between the icons. Multiple links have been made where necessary. This activity helps to stimulate pupils' thinking and learning prior to writing up the experiment. Inspiration is designed to re-format these ideas into a more structured form if desired, or this mind map can be saved as it is.

In Figure 8.4 a number of threads are shown; not just that iron and sulphur combine to create iron sulphide, but also what the process involves and what equipment is necessary. Inspiration can also be set to take each idea and expand it with additional notes, creating a structured writing frame for pupils to follow.

From this more structured screen it is possible to switch over to an Outline view where each point is listed in the same order but can be expanded upon to form a more complete text.

The last step in the process is to click on the 'Transfer' button, whereupon everything is exported to a word processor such as Word. Here the structured diagram and the outline are pasted into a new document ready to be polished into a completed piece of work. In a number of straightforward steps the brainstorm of ideas and icons can become a write-up of the experiment (Figure 8.5).

A similar idea of linking concepts can be found in the 'Visual Thesaurus' from TAG Learning. This gives a very visual representation of a chosen word and the

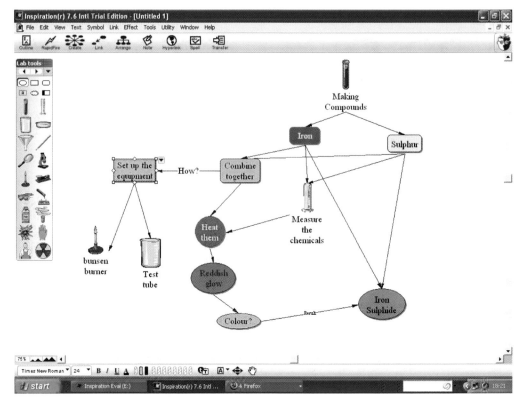

Figure 8.3 Brainstorm about the experiment

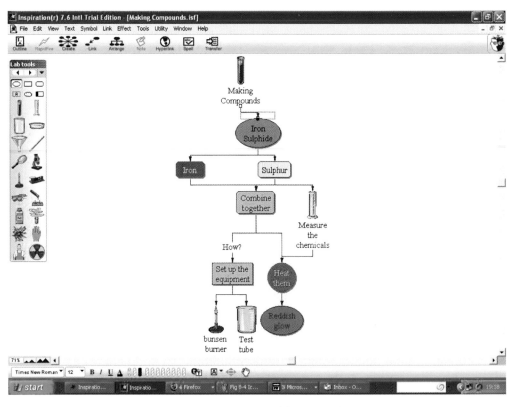

Figure 8.4 Icons rearranged for writing frame

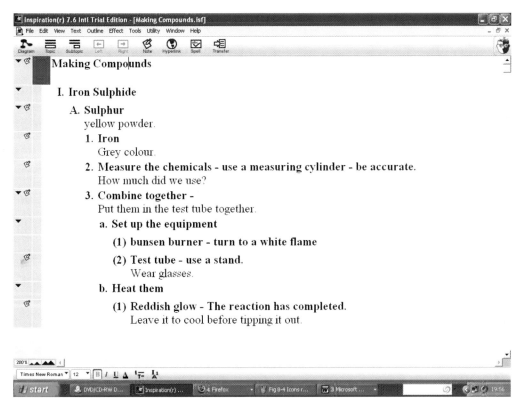

Figure 8.5 Point viewed as an outline

links it has to many others. Just like a traditional thesaurus, words with a similar meaning are shown and related to it. However, unlike a traditional thesaurus, everything is shown in a three-dimensional representation with lines linking words into a slowly revolving web that brings all the words into focus in turn. Any word can be pulled into the centre to research other associations. Throughout, there are definitions given on pop-up boxes and listed by parts of speech in the left-hand bar.

The representation is seemingly simple, the links between words made obvious and the various nuances disappearing off along different threads of meaning, all of which can be turned, pulled and stretched just like language can be. By presenting these links visually it helps reinforce their association cognitively.

The word 'compound' can be a mixture of chemicals or a group of buildings surrounded by a barrier. In the following example (Figure 8.6), key vocabulary has been chosen from a Year 9 History class on the topic of the Cold War. 'Conflict' is one of the key words that can have different levels of meaning. In this context it may mean actual fighting or it could be a struggle of ideologies and beliefs.

This program offers the opportunity to explore language. Rather like flicking through a dictionary and finding yourself being led down various routes, the Visual Thesaurus allows you to wander down linguistic avenues, linking and discussing as you go. All the words visited are recorded in the 'History' section at the bottom-right part of the screen, so it is always possible to get back to the task of researching and understanding the first word you looked for.

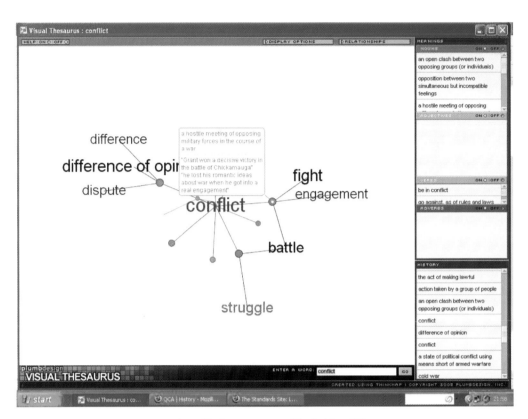

Figure 8.6 'Conflict' as represented in the Visual Thesaurus

Another tool for developing conceptual understanding of the language of a subject is Developing Tray from 2Simple Software. This can be viewed as a somewhat sophisticated version of the game 'Hangman', but that would be missing the real power of this program. Essentially, text is put up on screen with some or all of the letters missing. These are replaced by dashes or, for really challenging exercises, simply left blank. Words can be removed at a given frequency, individually selected ones can be missed or up to 20 of the most common letters omitted. The thinking behind the program is that the printed words are less important than their meaning. By removing the words, pupils are able to focus on the language and the concepts they are trying to convey. Paradoxically, this can mean that greater attention is given to decoding it while trying to make sense of it. It is a program that involves speaking and listening as well as reading and writing.

A related History class studying the development of world politics since the Second World War might study the Universal Declaration of Human Rights. In Developing Tray, this could look something like Figure 8.7.

Here only the first Article has been put up. The word 'declaration' has been left visible to give pupils a clue to the sort of text this would be. They would immediately have a sense of the grammar of the piece, that it may be forthright and didactic. The class would have been warmed up through discussion of the formation of the United Nations and its purpose. While they may not know the exact

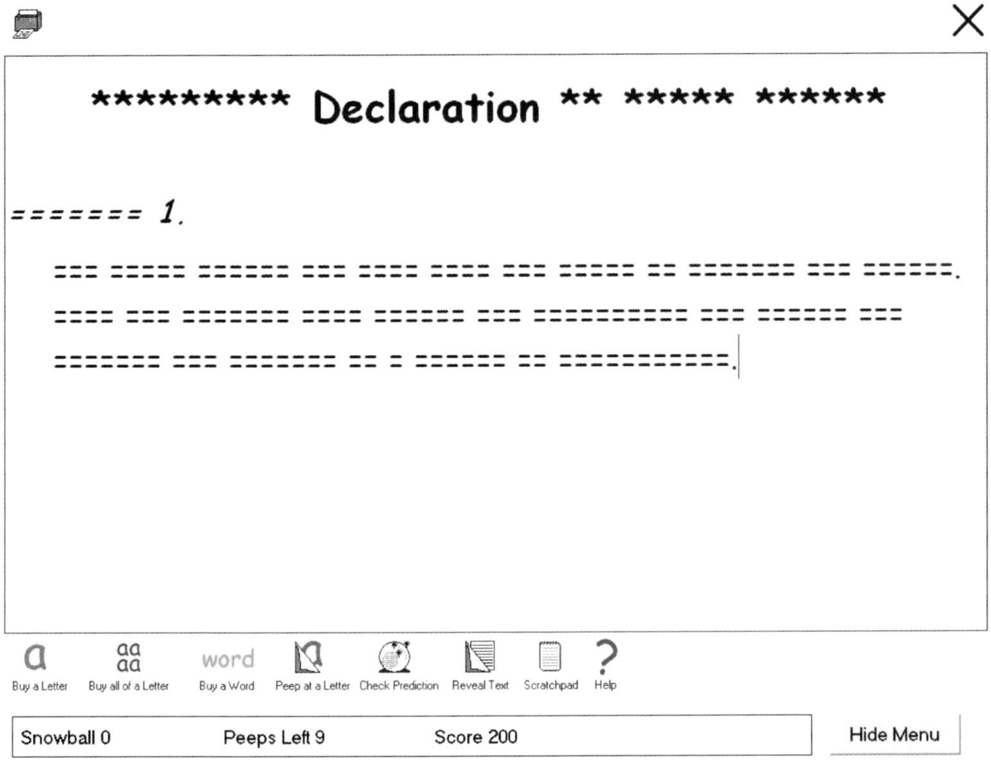

Figure 8.7 The Universal Declaration of Human Rights in Developing Tray

language of the text they could begin to propose the rights they believe should underpin such an organisation.

Developing Tray has tools to help move the exercise on if necessary by 'buying' words or letters, by 'peeping' at them and by checking predictions as you go. As the text is discovered, or uncovered, so the authors' beliefs will be revealed along with their ideals and hopes for the postwar world more powerfully than simply reading it. The pupils will have been through a process of choosing words and considering their meaning just as the world's representatives did over fifty years ago, when they came up with:

Universal Declaration of Human Rights

Article 1.

All human beings are born free and equal in dignity and rights. They are endowed with reason and conscience and should act towards one another in a spirit of brotherhood.

(United Nations General Assembly, 10 December 1948)

Developing Tray was designed to be used by groups, for pupils working together to construct understanding and meaning and to share their thoughts. This process can shift the model of learning from one where the teacher is delivering content to one where he or she is facilitating learning, which can be both exhilarating and challenging. However, it is an approach that can bring significant rewards to both pupils and staff.

A similar method of thinking about language can be achieved through the use of cloze exercises. Teaching can happen through determining what the missing words might be and understanding gauged by pupils' responses. One such program is ClozePro from Crick Software. This company's first product was the renowned Clicker, which works on the basis of writing by choosing words from a selection in a grid at the bottom of the screen. ClozePro grew out of it.

The program works by creating an exercise in an editing section. Here text can be typed in or copied and pasted. In a similar way to Developing Tray, there are a number of options for how text can be removed; the difference is that here words can be made available for pupils to select from and use in the piece. This would, typically, be by an on-screen grid or using drop-down lists. Various presentation methods are possible, with lists changing or words being removed once used. While essentially conceived as a means of creating literacy exercises for pupils, it lends itself well to working on a whiteboard. Here Article 1 of the United Nations Declaration of Human Rights is again used, but this time only key words are missing and these are offered in drop-down lists (Figure 8.8).

As can be seen, incorrect answers can be inserted. In this instance the teacher would use these responses as teaching points. When used individually the final

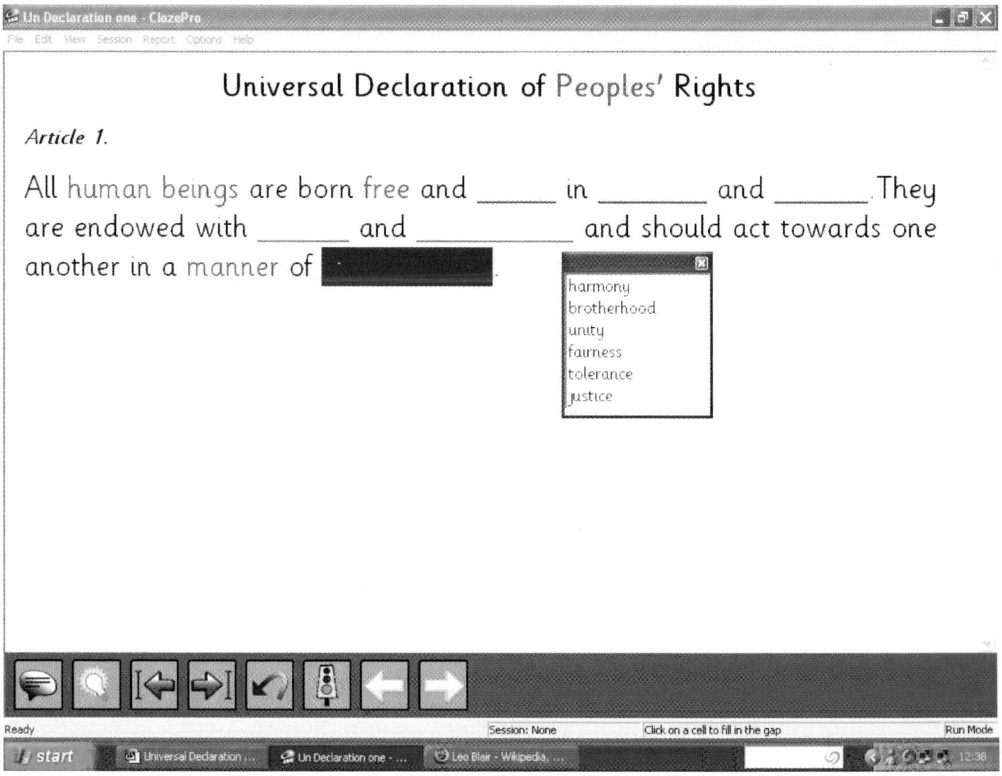

Figure 8.8 The United Nations Declaration of Human Rights in ClozePro

product can be printed out along with a report on how many answers were given correctly. There are also hints built in that can offer additional support, if appropriate, such as offering letters or showing a blurred outline of the word.

What ClozePro offers is an opportunity to focus on key vocabulary in a group. Following discussion, pupils can complete the exercise themselves or undertake a related activity, such as researching the actual text or rewriting it in their own words, or considering whether it is still relevant in the modern world.

Much of this way of learning – pupils creating their own understanding and making sense of the world in their own way – is associated with the constructivist ideas of Vygotsky and Piaget. These are very much evident in education and underpin the development of certain computer programs, the most famous of which is Logo.

Logo is a programming language that is best known as a means of controlling an on-screen pointer – usually called a turtle – to draw various shapes and designs. It is most commonly found in maths or ICT lessons. In the former, it can be used for teaching many mathematical concepts such as geometry, graphing and even trigonometry. In the latter, it can be used to teach programming to produce a range of results including following routes or making music. It is sufficiently flexible to be used from early childhood through to postgraduate level.

There are a number of Logo-based programs on the market. There is also one called MSWLogo that can be downloaded free-of-charge from the internet (www.softronix.com). Many of the commands are common to all versions. Some commercial versions include more pre-prepared elements or make the programming aspect more obvious through the way they are presented, using flowcharts or graphics for instance.

In the example in Figure 8.9 MSWLogo is being used to draw a house.

Here the Status panel is visible to show various aspects of the program, but most importantly the position of the turtle on the screen. The Editor panel is also visible as this is where procedures, strings of commands, are written. As can be seen, the door of the house appears to be falling off. One way to find out what the problem is is to use the Step button. With this depressed each command is shown on-screen before it is executed. This way it is possible to isolate the fault and ask the class what to do to correct it.

Logo in all its forms is a powerful tool for teaching logical, step-by-step thinking and problem-solving. When teaching geometry, angles, lengths of sides and number of repeats can all be altered to demonstrate fundamental principles such as the number of degrees in any geometric shape. The following coding will allow you to create a polygon with any number of sides of any length:

```
to polygon :length :sides
repeat :sides [fd :length rt 360.0/:sides]
end
```

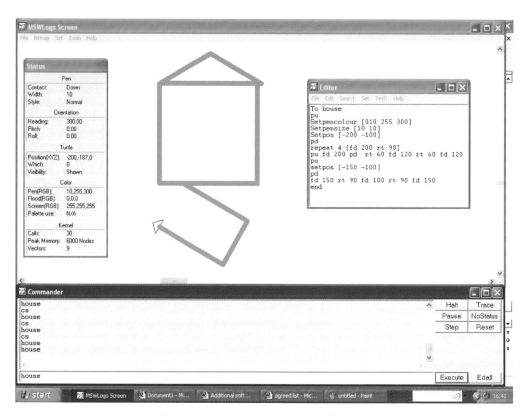

Figure 8.9 Drawing a house using MSWLogo

So to create a dodecagon with sides of length 100 simply type 'polygon 100 12'. A 'circle' can be made by creating a shape with 360 sides.

When it comes to ICT, giving the turtle commands and making it act as the students want is a valuable lesson in control technology, often forming part of a wider scheme of work that may include the use of robots. One of the most common hands-on tools used is Lego's Robolab. Based on a programmable brick with three inputs and three outputs, command procedures are built up on-screen and then transmitted to the robot through an infrared link. It is, however, possible to emulate the actions of these robots through the on-line version of Robolab (www.robolabonline.com).

The advantage of this version is that not just the programming but also the outcomes can be viewed and shared on the interactive whiteboard. Pupils can contribute to the programming as a whole class, or work in small groups and pairs, taking it in turns to demonstrate their suggestions, perhaps trying them out on their own computers first.

In the example in Figure 8.10 the buggy needs to be parked in a particular bay.

The animation first of all demonstrates the required action, then the user opens the Design Program tab and tries to get the buggy to follow the same path. In this case the buggy simply needs to turn in a confined space without touching the dark grey walls. If this happens the buggy explodes (Figure 8.11).

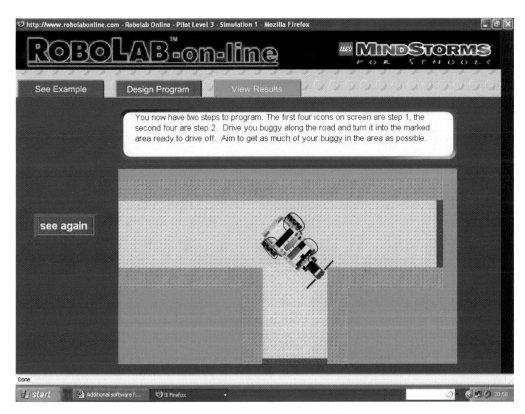

Figure 8.10 The demonstration screen in Robolab

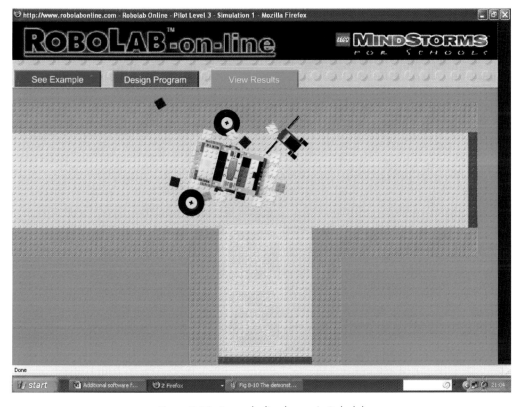

Figure 8.11 An exploding buggy in Robolab

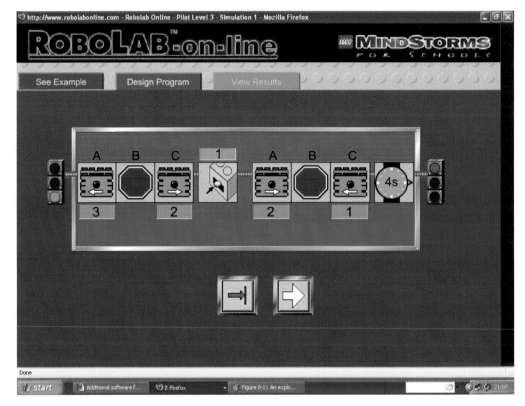

Figure 8.12 Programming the buggy in Robolab online

The programming in Robolab is graphical, that is icons are used to represent the different components, the motors and the sensors. The wheels turn in the direction of the arrows, so to go forward or back requires them to be pointed in opposite directions. They move at a given rate until an event, a timer or a sensor moves the program onto the next element (Figure 8.12).

While this method of programming seems less sophisticated than that of Logo, pupils can get involved in the process more quickly as there are no special commands or routines to learn. The graphics show what each step entails and adjustments are all done by clicking on the relevant box and choosing another component or variable. There is considerable potential for collective problem-solving that can engage the whole class. Just like working with the actual buggies the models can become quite sophisticated and include simulations such as fairground rides and traffic lights.

A further example of collective problem-solving in a different aspect of the curriculum is 'Life Skills – Traveller's Cheque' from Learning and Teaching Scotland (Figure 8.13). Designed for older pupils with learning difficulties the program simulates planning and preparing to go on holiday. Apart from choosing a destination, users have to get a job, open a bank account, go shopping and manage a budget. This software cannot be regarded as open, however. While there is some room for choice in respect of where to go and what to do, there is no control over the content by the teacher. The teacher's role here is to guide the students and

Figure 8.13 Visiting the travel agent's in Life Skills – Traveller's Cheque

make sure, through discussion of the decisions taken and the mistakes made, that learning is taking place.

Although the program is addressed to an individual user it is really designed to rehearse situations, promote discussion and practise decision-making. Pupils working as a group can provide a valuable resource for each other, offering different perspectives and alternative proposals for action, all with underlying reasons that will arise from personal understanding and values. While the closed nature of this game limits the teacher's options to adapt it to their class, it also means that some of the harsher realities of life, like missing the plane and not getting a holiday, affect everyone equally. It is fair and impartial in its judgements; it is also well presented with a clean, uncluttered appearance and with all the buttons at the bottom of the board.

As stated at the beginning of this chapter, good whiteboard software generally puts the teacher in control of the learning by giving him/her tools that are otherwise not available. Sometimes, however, closed environments can work well; it is the teacher and his/her capacity to engender learning that makes the difference in either case. The tools are only as good as the person using them.

Where to get help and find additional resources

Help, lesson resources, case studies and research reports can be found on many websites. Those listed below are a selection of those useful to secondary teachers. Unless otherwise stated, all resources are free.

IWB manufacturers' websites

1. Promethean's website has an area for users of their software. Go to www.prometheanworld.com/uk/, then click on the link to KS3/4 Resources in the Quick Links section. This contains resources contributed by teachers, teaching tips, resources for students with English as a second language, links to museum websites, and much more.

2. Downloads of the latest version of the software can be obtained from www.smart-uk.co.uk. Details of SMARTBoard software and hardware are available at www.smarttech.com/. Additional software, teaching resources, web resources, research reports and professional development opportunities can also be accessed from edcompass.smarttech.com/. Other resources, software downloads, training and support, and research reports are available at smarteducation.cant.ac.uk/.

3. Downloads of software updates, technical support and teaching resources for the StarBoard can be found at www.cambridgeboard.com.

4. Further details of Mimio software and portable interactive whiteboard systems can be obtained from www.mimio.com.

Sites directly supported by the DfES

1. Becta (British Educational Communications and Technology Agency), the ICT wing of the DfES, has many resources. These range from booklets on how to get the most out of your IWB to what research says about IWB use, to subject-specific booklets. Find out what they have at www.ictadvice.org.uk/.

2. At www.curriculumonline.gov.uk/ you can access everything offered by the Curriculum Online website. Some of this is free, some is not, but can be bought with e-learning credits. Evaluations of resources are published five times a year in *The Guardian*'s Evaluate supplement. Search under your subject and interactive whiteboards to find appropriate content.

3. The Standards Site of the DfES has many numeracy resources, some of which are suitable for secondary use, which can be used on an IWB. These can be downloaded from www.standards.dfes.gov.uk/numeracy/publications/. Their latest resources can be found at www.standards.dfes.gov.uk/primary/teachingresources/.

Good websites for teaching with whiteboards

There are probably two things you will use the internet for while teaching with a whiteboard: content for lessons and answers to questions that arise during them. Below are a number of sites that do one or both of these things.

www.multimap.com provides maps across the globe. Choose a country and type in a place name or post code and it will appear. Available at 13 different scales. Some areas have aerial photos available that can be overlaid with a map – great for getting across the concept of a graphical representation of a real situation.

www.howstuffworks.com doesn't just provide answers about how objects work but also diverse topics such as hypnosis or the papacy.

www.wikipedia.org is an on-line encyclopaedia built from contributions by people across the globe, so it is constantly expanding. And users, including school students, are welcome to make contributions to it.

www.cia.gov is host to 'The World Factbook', a very comprehensive list of facts about every recognised country in the world.

www.dictionary.com checks definitions from more than one source. Also has a thesaurus.

www.learningcurve.gov.uk The education section of The National Archives.

www.Stats4schools.gov.uk Statistics about all sorts of things for use in schools; includes large datasets for interrogation.

www.nationalgallery.org.uk provides access to famous paintings on-line.

www.bl.uk The British Library on-line – samples of books with articles and samples of their pages.

www.bbc.co.uk/history/multimedia_zone Interactive area of the BBC History site. Includes 3D representations of historic places such as a sixteenth-century London Bridge and a First World War trench.

www.bbc.co.uk/science/humanbody/body Similar resources from the Science area of the BBC website.

www.gimp-savvy.com Thousands of copyright-free images from US government agencies such as NASA and the Fisheries and Wildlife Service.

www.geoimages.berkeley.edu/wwp.html Panoramic photos (can be turned through 360 degrees) from across the globe.

www.essentialnormanconquest.com Lots of resources including panoramas of the battlefield.

www.becta.org.uk Advice on all sorts of issues when using ICT in teaching, including interactive whiteboards in secondary schools.

Other websites

Websites come and go. It is difficult and very time-consuming to keep track of them. If you want information or an image for a particular topic, a search on www.google.com is a good place to start. There are also useful books, such as *Red Hot ICT Websites* by Hilary Lewis, published by Letts. This list includes a few that I have found useful.

1. The BBC website, www.bbc.co.uk/, has a vast wealth of material which can be used to bring lessons to life.

2. The British Pathé Archive, www.britishpathe.com/, has thousands of hours of digitised newsreel which is freely available for schools to use.

3. The Caret website (University of Cambridge) has on-line brainteasers and puzzles at www.puzzling.caret.cam.ac.uk/. At www.revolution.caret.cam.ac.uk/, there are interactive on-line resources in the biological sciences, and www.humanfactory.caret.cam.ac.uk/ is a 3D game in which students can explore the human digestive system.

4. The Converse website at www.aspirations.english.cam.ac.uk has innovative resources for secondary English lessons.

5. The Dorset LEA ICT team has prepared a web page – www.dorset.rmplc.co.uk/dornum/default.htm – which is full of useful links for maths lessons. Some are specifically aimed at KS1 and KS2, but many will be useful to secondary schools as well.

6. The Keele University Interactive Whiteboards website, www.keele.ac.uk/depts/ed/iaw/, contains research papers and information and resources for using an IWB in the maths lesson.

7. The Nrich website at www.nrich.maths.org has a wide range of mathematical problems, games and activities, many of which would be very suitable for use on an IWB.

8. Teachers at Parkside Community College, Cambridge, are developing materials for IWB use, some of which are available from the school website www.che.e2bn.leas/c99/schools/che/dtabase/index.php.

9. The Review Project website has help and advice for IWB users, guides for each subject area and case studies on IWB use. Access these at www.thereviewproject.org/index.htm.

10. Jersey maths teacher, Rory Steel, has a great collection of IWB resources available on his website, www.rsmaths.com/.

11. At www.teachit.co.uk/ you can find a library of free English teaching resources.

12. The Teem (teachers evaluating educational multimedia) website, at www.teem.org.uk/ has many IWB resources which can be found by putting 'whiteboard' into the Search facility.

Copyright

Most pictures on the internet will not be in the public domain, and there will be copyright restrictions on their use. Many websites allow free use of their resources for educational purposes, but you should check to see who owns the copyright and what restrictions there are before using a photo. If it is not clear that educational use is allowed, you can always e-mail the copyright owner and ask for permission.

Reference table for AS2

Function	Icon or on-screen	Menu
Background colour		Page Edit>Properties>Appearance>Page Colour
Backgrounds		Right toolbar>Resource Library>Shared backgrounds
Calculator		Floating toolbar>Special Tools>Calculator
Clear Screen		Floating toolbar
Clipart		Right toolbar>Resource Library>Images
Clock		Floating toolbar>Special Tools>Clock
Copy object to clipboard		M>Edit>Copy to clipboard
Copy object		Object Edit>Copy or M>Edit>Copy
Delete object		Object Edit>Delete
	Drag into dustbin	
Duplicate object		Object Edit>Duplicate or M>Edit>Duplicate
Fill		Floating toolbar>Fill
Flipchart Recorder		Floating toolbar>Power Tools>Flipchart Recorder
Fraction tool		Floating toolbar>Power Tools>Fraction Tool
Grids		Right toolbar>Resource Library>Shared Grids

Grouping objects		Select objects to be grouped>Object Edit>Properties>Identification>Group
Handwriting recognition		Floating toolbar>Recognition Tool
Help		Floating toolbar>Promethean man>Help or right-click on a tool or icon
Hyperlinks		Object Edit>Properties>Action
Mask grid		Page Edit>Mask grid
New flipchart		Floating toolbar>Promethean man>Flipchart>New
Next page		Right toolbar>Right arrow
On-screen keyboard		Floating toolbar>Power Tools>Keyboard
Open flipchart		Floating toolbar>Promethean man>Flipchart>Open
Page organiser		Right toolbar>Page organiser
Page selector		Right toolbar>Page selector
Paste object from the clipboard		M>Edit>Paste from clipboard
Paste		Object Edit>Paste or M>Edit>Paste
Pens, highlighters and erasers		Floating toolbar
Previous page		Right toolbar>Left arrow
Print flipchart		Floating toolbar>Promethean man>Print
Protractor		Floating toolbar>Power Tools>Protractor
Redo		Floating toolbar
Reset the page		Right toolbar>Page reset
Resizing an object	Select and use resizing handles	Object Edit>+ or –
Resource library		Right toolbar
Ruler		Floating toolbar>Power Tools>Ruler
Save annotations		Floating toolbar>Promethean man>ACTIVextras>ACTIVmarker

Function	Icon or on-screen	Menu
Save flipchart		Floating toolbar>Promethean man>Save
Shape Recognition		Floating toolbar>Recognition Tool
Shapes		Floating toolbar>Pen>right click
Snap to grid		Page Edit>Snap to grid
Snapshot		Floating toolbar>Screen Capture
Sound		Object Edit>Properties>Action> or right toolbar>Resource Library>Shared Sounds
Text editor		Object Edit>+ or – icons to resize, Object Edit>T for other editing
Toolbox Customise		Floating toolbar>Promethean man>Toolbox Customise
Typed text		Floating toolbar>T
Undo		Floating toolbar
Web browser		Floating toolbar>Power Tools>Web browser

Reference table for SMARTBoard

Function	Icon/on-screen	Menu	Key board
Area capture	Floating tools		
Attachments		View>Attachments	Alt 3
Background colour	Right-click>Set Background Color	Format>background color	
Calculator	Floating tools		
Clear page	Right-click> Clear Page Page Sorter> Clear Page	Edit>Clear Page	Ctrl L
Clipart		View>Gallery Insert>Picture/ Template>Gallery	Alt 2
Copy	Select object> Menu>Copy	Edit>Copy	Ctrl C
Creative pen	Toolbar or floating tools		

Function	Icon/on-screen	Menu	Key board
Customize Tools	Floating tools		
Cut	Select object> Menu>Cut	Edit>Cut	Ctrl X
Editing text	Double click on text		
Eraser	Toolbar, floating tools or pen tray	Draw>Eraser	
Full-screen view		View>Full screen	Alt ENTER
Handwriting recognition	Select freehand text>Menu		
Highlighter	Toolbar or floating tools		
Hyperlink	Attachments	Attachments> Insert>Insert Hyperlink Insert>Hyperlink	
Insert blank page		Insert>Blank page	
Keyboard	Floating tools or Start Center		
New notebook	Toolbar Start Center tools	File>New	Ctrl N
Next page		View>Next Page	Page Down
Open notebook		File>Open	Ctrl O
Page navigation	Page Sorter	View>Page Sorter	Alt 1

Paste		Edit>Paste	Ctrl V
Pen		Draw>Pen	
	Toolbar, floating tools, pen tray or finger		
Previous page		View>Previous page	Page Up
Print		File>Print	Ctrl P
Redo		Edit>Redo	Ctrl Y
	Toolbar or floating tools		
Resizing objects	Select, then drag on bottom-right circle		
Save		File>Save	Ctrl S
Screen Capture toolbar		View>Screen Capture	
	Toolbar or floating tools		
Screen Capture			
	Floating tools		
Screen shade		View>Screen Shade	
Shapes		Draw menu	
Spotlight			
	Floating tools		
Start Centre			
Typed text			
	Start typing		
Undo		Edit>Undo	Ctrl Z
	Toolbar or floating tools		
Video player			
	Start Center tools		
Video recorder			
	Start Center tools		
Zoom/magnifier		View>Zoom	
	Toolbar or floating tools		

Reference table for StarBoard

Function	Icon/on-screen	Menu
Activate grid		View>Grid>Activate Grid
Background colour		Settings>Option Setting>View
Backgrounds		Documents>Templates
Clear		Edit>Clear
Clipart		Tools>Clipart
Copy		Edit>Copy
Cover/Uncover Sheet		View>Cover/Uncover Sheet
Cut		Edit>Cut
Delete an object		Edit>Delete
Eraser		Tools>Eraser
Favourites		Documents>Favourites
Font size	Pull out text box to required size or resize using handles	
Grids		View>Grid
Handwriting recognition		Settings>FEP>On
Hide/show grid		View>Grid>Show Grid Line
Highlighters, brushes		Tools>Colour Palette

Hyperlinks	Type full URL into a text box	
Intelli-pen		Tools>Intelli-pen
Keyboard		Mode>Accessories>On-Screen Keyboard
Linked files		Documents>Favourites>Add favourite
New flipchart	Delete current content, and use Save As	
New page		Documents>New blank page
Next page		View>Next page
Page organiser		View>Page List
Page selector		View>Page List
Paste		Edit>Paste
Pen and eraser width		Tools>Pen Width
Pen		Tools>Pen
Previous page		View>Previous page
Print flipchart		Mode>Print
Redo		Edit>Redo
Resizing an object	Select and use resizing handles	
Save annotations		Edit>Paste in MS-Office (with Settings>Option Settings>General> Capture Desktop and write on it selected)
Save flipchart		View>Page List
Screen capture		Mode>Accessories>ScreenCapture
Screenblock		Mode>Accessories>Screenblock
Shape Recognition		Tools>Intelli-pen
Shapes		Tools>Objects
Stopwatch		Mode>Accessories>Stopwatch
Text editor	Double-click on text	Tools>Object Property
Text		Tools>Objects>Text
Undo		Edit>Undo

Index

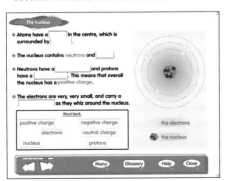